Whatsoever You Do:

Helping Students Think Deeply About Service Experiences

Edited by Martin Connell, S.J.
and Christiane Connors

**A Guide
for and by
Christian Service
Learning
Practitioners**

National Catholic Educational Association

Cover photo of C&O Canal, Washington, DC by Christiane Connors

National Catholic Educational Association
1077 30th Street, NW, Suite 100
Washington, DC 20007-3852
800-711-6232 • www.ncea.org

ISBN 1-55833-441-6
Part No. SDV-21-1439

Our lives are really all that belong to us.... Only by giving our lives do we find life.

Our lives are really
all that belong to us....
Only by giving our lives
do we find life.

— César Chávez

Table of Contents

How to Get the Most from This Book

Christiane Connors

How often do high school students *feel* deeply about their service experiences, but do not *think* deeply about the experiences? Ideally, a high school service program encourages students to feel and think deeply about their community service initiatives to avoid what T.S. Eliot (1968) described: "We had the experience, but missed the meaning." Without the encouragement and structures that support deep consideration, contemplation, and reflection on their experiences, service initiatives cannot effectively help students grasp the meaning behind their actions and participate in service mindfully. In this regard, service-learning programs are countercultural not only by serving as an antidote to cultural values that encourage the pursuit of self-interest but also by providing a respite from the fast-paced and action-oriented ways of being in the world that predominate daily life in the United States. Using service as a way to help our students make sense of what it means to be a Catholic Christian, however, requires attention to both foundational and practical components of a service program. School leaders must continually ask: *What do we want to develop in our service-learning program? What do we hope students learn that will stick with them after they leave our school? What can we do to develop habits of critically reflecting on experiences in order to imagine a better world?*

This book is *for* practitioners and *by* practitioners who are or have been involved in Catholic high school service programs and who have demonstrated skill in addressing foundational and practical challenges. Each featured author has created and fostered "some moral energy, moral passion, moral intelligence [among their students] which says that we all can be larger than ourselves and to be able to ask the questions that are so crucial for these times" (Brown, 2004).

The chapters that follow present principles that mark effective service-learning programs in Catholic schools. The chapters consider such things as the virtue of solidarity, the relationship between charity and justice, protesting as service, service and leadership, the relationship of service to the devout life, the relationship of service to other characteristics of the Church (like community and worship). These and other core themes have foundational and practical concerns attached to them. Reflecting on these principles, the authors share their insights about promising practices and strategies for the benefit of their colleagues in Catholic schools nationwide.

Each chapter includes three signposts: PRINCIPLE, STRATEGY, and TRY TOMORROW (adapted from Pollock, 2008) that offer readers helpful guidance in getting the most from the book.

- PRINCIPLE invites participants to consider what **core principle** the chapter addresses: What is essential to the principle the author examines that students ought to learn? For example, what ways of teaching students about the Catholic notions of justice seem the most likely to be successful?
- STRATEGY invites participants to consider the **general strategies** the author suggests through his or her examples, shared wisdom and conclusion: How can staff tailor the author's plans of action to meet the specific needs of the program? For example, which action steps suggested in the chapter will help students in your school understand how service, charity, and justice are related? Which will not?
- TRY TOMORROW invites participants to consider specific steps to achieve real and meaningful changes. How can specific activities develop habits of critical reflection on experiences that encourage students to re-imagine a better world? For example, what specific questions would help students deepen their thinking of their experience, here and beyond?

The signposts offer various facets of the principles for consideration and provide entry points for important conversations about service-learning among different constituents, including students, parents, school administrators, board members, local community and business leaders. The questions can assist personal and group reflection, on-the-job staff development, planning meetings, program reviews and other gatherings aimed at establishing or improving a school's service program.

Effective service-learning programs foster the pursuit of knowledge by encouraging students to live in the question and to see the horizon of service learning as an invitation rather than a limit. In a beautiful passage on inspiration and knowledge, Polish poet Wislawa Szymbroska, a Nobel laureate in literature, remarked:

> Whatever inspiration is, it is born from a continuous 'I don't know.'… Any knowledge that doesn't lead to new questions quickly dies out: it fails to maintain the temperature required for sustaining life…This is why I value that little phrase 'I don't know' so highly. It's small, but it flies on mighty wings. It expands our lives to include the spaces within us as well as those outer expanses in which our tiny Earth hangs suspended. (excerpted by Brown, 2004)

High school service programs ought to value the phrase "I don't know" as they encourage students to feel and think deeply about their service experiences. We will have served our students well if at the end of their service experience they are left with unanswered questions *and* the willingness to pray and reflect on them. Our hope and prayer is that the pages that follow will serve to help you create an effective service program if your school is starting a program or serve to enhance an existing program. Ultimately, we hope that your consideration of the foundational and practical components presented in the chapters will serve you in assisting your students to imagine a better world through their service.

Resources

Brown, T. (2004). *Great ideas, gentle as doves: Reflections on Catholic social teaching.* Baltimore: Resonant Publishing.

Eliot, T.S. (1968). *Four quartets.* London: Harvest Books.

Pollock, M. (2008). *Everyday antiracism: Getting real about race in school.* New York: The New Press.

Chapter 1

Service Learning: Formation in Practical Christianity
Michael G. Lee, S.J.

When it was evening, the disciples approached Jesus and said, "This is a deserted place and it is already late; dismiss the crowds so that they can go to the villages and buy food for themselves." Jesus said to them, "There is no need for them to go away; give them some food yourselves." But they said to him, "Five loaves and two fish are all we have here." Then he said, "Bring them here to me," and he ordered the crowds to sit down on the grass. Taking the five loaves and the two fish, and looking up to heaven, he said the blessing, broke the loaves, and gave them to the disciples, who in turn gave them to the crowds. They all ate and were satisfied, and they picked up the fragments left over – twelve wicker baskets full. Those who ate were about five thousand. (Mt 14:13-21)

Every Friday in Omaha, a group of ten Catholic high school sophomores and their teacher takes a school van across the city to the Open Door Mission to spend the morning making sandwiches for homeless people. They donate the lunch meat for the sandwiches. Later, divided into teams of five, the sophomores ride the circuit in the mission's vans to deliver the sandwiches directly to homeless people on the street. In the span of a single school day, ten sophomores and one teacher have implemented Jesus' command, "Give them some food yourselves."

In a practical, down-to-earth way, the teacher and students work together to meet a pressing human need; and they have a safe, supervised, first-hand experience feeding hungry and homeless people. Through their service to and with the poor, students fulfill their sophomore retreat requirement and learn about poverty in the local community along with their teacher. They work together to give public witness to the mission of a Catholic high school. When these students advance to junior year, their common experience of direct contact with the poor provides a sense of purpose and the context for their study of Catholic social teaching (CST) (Smith, Sullivan & Shortt, 2006, p.11). By partnering on a "Streets of the City" project like this one with a social service agency like Open Door Mission, any Catholic high school can enhance its curriculum and provide its students and teachers with a hands-on learning experience in practical Christianity that makes it possible for homeless people to have their daily bread at the same time (Bordelon & Phillips, 2006; S. Joyce-Whipp, personal communication, December 18, 2008).

A hands-on learning experience in practical Christianity recognizes the experience of members of the believing community over the ages. There is an ancient principle of the Church that states that the rule of prayer is at the same time the rule of belief (in Latin: *lex orandi, lex credendi*). The principle recognizes both that the early Church had a tradition of worship that provided a structure as it began to articulate more systematic theological accounts of the experience of salvation in Christ Jesus and that worship and belief are intricately bound. The principle acknowledges that believers do no experience their everyday faith life as partitioned into discrete sections of doctrine, worship, service, etc., but that they rather experience their faith as something more whole, more integral. This chapter explores how service (*diakonia*) is rightly considered in the context of the everyday life of the believer (practical Christianity) by considering its relationship to teaching (*didache*), worship (*leiturgia*), announcing/witnessing to the Good News of salvation (*kerygma-martyria*), and community (*koinonia*).

Service's relationship with the other facets of the Christian life has implications for what service learning should look like as part of the religious formation of the next generation of believers at Catholic schools and in Catholic parishes. That is to say that service learning in a Catholic context should properly be conceived as part of catechesis, "the process of transmitting the Gospel, as the Christian community has received it, understands it, celebrates it, lives it and communicates it in many ways" (*General Directory for Catechesis* [GDC], para. 105).

The pages that follow provide an opportunity to look at service in light of the recently inaugurated renewal process in the Church in the United States that explores how culturally diverse Catholic teens can more effectively be formed in the faith. These renewal efforts are spearheaded in large part by the National Initiative on Adolescent Catechesis (NIAC), which has been supported by generous grants from the Lilly Endowment and an anonymous donor. Participants in NIAC have begun to draw important lessons from exemplary service programs at Catholic high schools, lessons that are helpful to anyone beginning a formal service learning program or renewing an established one.

Diakonia & Didache: **Service & Teaching**

Service programs at Catholic high schools can excel at putting the faith of Catholic teens in conversation with CST and with the world's pressing needs. In particular, service programs with a strong reflective component are a socially-engaged approach to adolescent faith formation and an effective means of encouraging a sense of purpose among adolescents. Researchers on the notion of *purpose* in adolescent development note that

> Young people who express purpose, in the sense of a dedication to causes greater than the self, show high degrees of religiosity, consolidated identities, and deeper senses of meaning than those who do not experience purpose. In addition, the value of purpose to the self continues well beyond the adolescent period – indeed, throughout the rest of the life-span. All of this suggests that purpose plays a positive role in self-development as well as a generative one for the person's contributions to society (Damon, Menon, & Bronk, 2003, p. 126).

Though purpose as such cannot be taught, the structuring resources for students to attain such a sense can be provided to them.

For instance, Laura Henning, an NIAC-affiliated author who serves as a theology instructor and the service learning coordinator at Bishop Kelly High School in Boise, Idaho, has noted how "hands-on, experience-based methodologies" that are a regular part of students' participation in meaningful liturgies and service and other campus ministry-sponsored activities provide them with resources to "become not just hearers of the Word, but doers as well (Lk 6:49)" (Henning, 2008). It might be said that purpose is more "caught" than "taught." It is for that reason that Henning calls on schools and parishes "to do a better job at linking young people to Catholic networks and finding for them men and women of faith who can be personal witnesses and mentors in discipleship" (Henning, 2008; see also Smith, 2005). "When leading by example," she notes, "school faculties show how Catholic values and belief can be lived throughout one's life" (Henning, 2008).

Purpose as it is understood here should not be confused with understandings of purpose presented in popular books like *The Purpose-Driven Life* (Warren, 2002). For Warren, purpose and determinism are practically synonymous: Every detail of life as it unfolds is the way God willed it from the beginning. As Baker (2006) notes, "It's as if allowing even the possibility of an event without God's written intention would undermine the whole thesis that life has a purpose" (p. 133). To find purpose in such a spirituality means putting on one's Sherlock Holmes cap and setting out with magnifier in hand searching for some "insight into what God was thinking eons ago when everything was worked out in such detail" (p. 134).

What our students need relative to purpose is reflection rather than detection. In order to be effective relative to assisting our students' growth in meaning – their search for purpose – good service learning programs offer ample opportunities for students to engage in theological reflection so that they "don't see these [service] opportunities simply as hoops to jump through" (Henning, 2008). *Theological reflection* as the term is used here means examining one's experience with the intention of acquiring knowledge about God and learning how to live a more Christian life. To engage in such reflection is to cultivate a habit of attentiveness (Yust & Anderson, 2006, pp. 158-159). Yust and Anderson (2006) suggest that by practicing methods of reflection consistently over a period of weeks students increase their ability to focus their attention during periods of personal and communal prayer as well as at times when engaged in sustained reflection on the intersection of daily life, service, scripture and tradition. A model for such reflection appears in the Appendix of this book.

Diakonia & Leiturgia: Service & Communal Prayer

Aristotle wrote so many years ago that virtues are habits rather than acts. *Diakonia* is a lifelong habit of engaging in Christian practices of service that foster on-going conversion and that favorably dispose a person to make a conscious, deliberate decision to follow Jesus Christ's example of a life lived in self-offering for the welfare of others. For Catholics, service concerns not only secular values of good citizenship and civic concern for the common good, but also discipleship. Service is a pathway for following Jesus. Rooted in the Gospel message and the Catholic Tradition, *diakonia* mediates Jesus Christ's active presence to a faith community, and he renders the community's service effective. It might be said that service is done to the glory of God the Father through Jesus, with Jesus, and in Jesus; in the unity of the Holy Spirit.

The close inter-relationship of communal prayer and service is deeply ingrained in the Catholic Tradition, especially the sacraments. The *Catechism of the Catholic Church* underscores the relationship between the two when it states that liturgy "refers not only to the celebration of divine worship but also to the proclamation of the Gospels and to active charity ... the service of God and neighbor" (para. 1070). An example might help to illustrate the Catholic understanding of this connection between service and worship. A group of parents from Dolores Mission Catholic Church, a poor, Anglo and Latino faith community in gang-disputed territory in East Los Angeles, California, regularly visits incarcerated teens at the nearby Central Juvenile Hall. Through years of visits that have included the parishioners' offering counsel to and praying with the incarcerated adolescents, these parents and their pastor have arrived at profound insights into the mystery of suffering and the meaning of Jesus' crucifixion. Their service has given them new reverence for God's healing mercy; that is, their service has moved them to worship just as their worship earlier had inspired their service.

The dynamic interrelationship of prayer and service articulates one of Jesus' most important teachings, the double commandment to love God and neighbor (Thavis, 2008). The Sacrament of Baptism initiates Christians into a community of faith that loves God and neighbor and is centered on the saving event of Jesus Christ's life, death, and resurrection. Baptism is God's free gift through water and the Holy Spirit by which the faithful enter into the death and resurrection of the Lord. It announces a universal call to holiness. Because most students arrive at Catholic high schools as baptized members of the community, they should be treated not only as objects of catechesis but also as "active subjects and protagonists of evangelization, and artisans of social renewal" (GDC, para.183). Catholic high schools' service programs offer an apprenticeship in Christian living that encourages purpose and an adult faith that embraces both serving the poor and divine worship as a member of a Catholic parish community.

The inter-relationship of prayer and service in Christ's name has deep roots in the life and curriculum of the Church; it is woven into the Catholic Tradition. For example, the gospels record "various accounts of the multiplication of the loaves and fishes, two each in the gospels of Mark and Matthew, and one each in the gospels of Luke and John" (*SMP College Study Bible*, 2006, p. 1499, n.1). Someone once remarked that the greater miracle followed the multiplication: The disciples actually shared the multiplied nourishment with others. Perhaps, in fact, the early Christian communities recognized that "learning to serve others rather than oneself does not come naturally to human beings. It has to be learned" (Waal, 1996, cited in Sikula & Sikula, 2005, p. 77). In any case, the ritual pattern, the fourfold action of taking, blessing, breaking, and distributing the bread, embedded in these gospel accounts makes clear that early Christian communities encountered the Risen Lord both in their Eucharistic celebrations and in their communal service to the widow, stranger, and the orphan. Programs of Christian formation for our youth that follow a similar pattern will assist them in living integrated lives in the community of believers.

Diakonia & Kerygma-Martyria: **Service & the Good News of Salvation**

In his encyclical *Deus Caritas Est*, Pope Benedict XVI (2005) wrote of three constitutive elements of the Church. "The Church's deepest nature," he wrote, "is expressed in her threefold responsibility: of proclaiming the word of God (*kerygma-martyria*), celebrating the sacraments (*leitourgia*), and exercising the ministry of charity (*diakonia*)" (para. 25).

Diakonia and *kerygma-martyria* are closely linked:

The Good News of the Kingdom of God, which proclaims salvation, includes a message of liberation for all, but especially for the poor. Jesus addressed his announcement of the kingdom principally to the frail, the vulnerable, the disabled, and the poor... (*National Directory for Catechesis* [NDC], p. 78).

We are held accountable to the story of God revealed in the life-giving mysteries of the life, death, and resurrection of Jesus Christ, whose preaching on the Kingdom reveals that God is not distant but is loving and present among us, offering us salvation, freeing us from sin, and bringing us into communion with him and all humanity (NDC, p. 79).

His teachings, miracles, and healings point to the presence of the Kingdom, and the Sermon on the Mount is the manifesto of this reign. In the Sermon on the Mount, Jesus declares the inauguration of God's changing the history of the world. In this regard, Christians are less concerned about what they ought to do as individuals to make history come out right for them and more concerned about Christ, who has already made history come out right (Hauerwas, 1989). Participation in service is an opportunity for students to witness (*martyria*) to the advent of the Kingdom of God. A line spoken by the character Angel of the eponymous television series of the early 2000s captures how in the Catholic view of things doing service witnesses to the Kingdom: "We live as though the world were as it should be to show it what it can be."

Diakonia & Koinonia: **Service & Community**

The integral relationship between service and community can be traced to apostolic times. We read in the Acts of the Apostles that

There was no needy person among them, for those who owned property or houses would sell them, bring the proceeds of the sale, and put them at the feet of the apostles, and they were distributed to each according to need. (Acts 4:34-36)

It is not possible for the Church to engage in service without a connection to the community. Maria Harris (1989) notes that as forms of pastoral and educational vocation, community and service are "essentially related" (p. 157); that is, each implicates the other.

For this reason, service is made more effective when it is done in the context of a faith community that seeks the help of God in seeing a service project through to its completion. Service and community are more clearly connected when a local Catholic high school or parish youth group participates in a service project or charitable activity aligned to a ministry of the Church

(GDC, para. 253). One important way to help students understand (that is, *learn*) the relationship of service and community is by tracing with them the Church's history of service from the ways the disciples participated in the healing ministry of Jesus to present-day social ministries of the Church.

The experience of service can assist students in coming to appreciate that people working together can undertake service projects that no single individual would ever attempt. Opportunities for service provided by Catholic schools and parishes provide an excellent opportunity for adolescents to think about the intersection of their Catholic faith, to learn about needs in the local community, and to appreciate the power of community to effect social change.

Conclusion

This chapter has examined the place of service in light of the *General Directory for Catechesis* and the U.S. Catholic Church's *National Initiative on Adolescent Catechesis* with special reference to service's relationship to other constitutive elements of the Church: *didache, leiturgia, kerygma-martyria, and koinonia.* As a result, this chapter has addressed to some degree all six tasks of catechesis identified in the GDC, including promoting knowledge of the faith, liturgical education, moral formation (service for the poor), teaching to pray, education for community life, and missionary initiation, especially in regard to *kerygma-martyria* and the Kingdom of God (GDC, paras. 85-87). The Catholic Church draws from its tradition in order to re-vitalize its approaches to educating U.S. Catholic teens in faith. With God's help on this path of renewal, those of us charged with the Christian formation of our youth in the U.S. Catholic Church strive to make our catechesis

a catechesis of grace, the love of God, which prompts our good works and by which we are saved...

a catechesis of the twofold commandment of charity: to love God above all things, and to love our neighbor as ourselves...

a catechesis of the Church in which the Christian life is received, nourished, and perfected in Christ.

This catechesis always begins and ends in Christ, who is "the way, the truth, and the life." (NDC, p. 158).

Discussion Questions

1. **Principle:** What ways of talking about service seem most likely to be successful in terms of understanding it as an integral part of Christian belief?

2. **Strategy:** What ways can you emphasize service learning as an experience of practical Christianity?

3. **Try tomorrow:** How do you distinguish Christian service from good citizenship and civic engagement?

Resources

Baker, T. (2006, February 24). Purpose-driven spirituality: How deep does Rick Warren go? *Commonweal*, (*133*) 4, 22-23.

Bordelon, T. D. & Phillips, I. (2006). Service-learning: What students have to say. *Active Learning in Higher Education, 7*, 143-153.

Catechism of the catholic church with modifications from the editio typica. (1997). New York: Doubleday.

Congregation for the Clergy. (1998). *General directory for catechesis.* Downloaded April 22, 2009 from http://www.vatican.va/roman_curia/congregations/cclergy/documents/rc_con_ccatheduc_doc_17041998_directory-for-catechesis_en.html

Damon, William, Jenni Mennon, and Kendall Cotton Bronk. (2003). The development of purpose during adolescence. *Applied Developmental Science, 7*(3), 119-128.

Harris, M. (1989). *Fashion me a people: Curriculum in the church.* Louisville, KY: Westminster John Knox Press.

Hauerwas, S. (1989). *Resident aliens: Life in the Christian colony.* Nashville, TN: Abingdon Press.

Henning, L. (2008). Forming disciples of Jesus in parish and school. Down-loaded April 22, 2009 from http://www.adolescentcatechesis.org/re-sources/documents/Henning_ParishSchool.pdf

Pope Benedict XVI. (2005). *Deus caritas est.* Downloaded April 22, 2009 from www.vatican.va/holy_father/benedict_xvi/encyclicals/documents/hf_ben-xvi_enc_20051225_deus-caritas-est_en.html

Saint mary's press college study Bible [NAB]. (2007).Winona, MN: Saint Mary's Press.

Sikula, J., & Sikula, A. (2005). Spirituality and service learning. *New Directions for Teaching and Learning, 104*, 75-81.

Smith, C., & Denton, M.L. (2005). *Soul searching: The religious and spiritual lives of american teenagers.* New York, NY: Oxford University Press.

Smith, D. I., Sullivan, J., & Shortt., J. (2006). Introduction: Connecting spirituality, justice, and pedagogy. *Journal of Education & Christian Belief, 10*, 7-21.

Thavis, John. (2008, October). Pope closes synod, says bible is put into practice through service. *Catholic News Service.* Downloaded April 22, 2009 from http://www.catholicnews.com/data/stories/cns/0805457.htm

United States Conference of Catholic Bishops. (2005). *National directory for catechesis.* Washington, D.C.: USCCB.

Waal, F. (1996). *Good natured: The origins of right and wrong in humans and other animals.* Cambridge, MA: Harvard University Press.

Warren, R. (2002). *The purpose-driven life: What on earth am I here for?* Grand Rapids, MI: Zondervan.

Yust, K.M., & Anderson, E. B, (2006). *Taught by God: Teaching and spiritual formation.* St. Louis, MO: Chalice Press.

Chapter 2

Solidarity: From Other to Sister and Brother

Martin T. Connell, S.J.

There is a frequently told story about a rabbi and his students. One day the rabbi asked his students how the hour of dawn could be determined. "How do we know," he asked, "when the night has ended and day has arrived?" One of the students suggested that it was when a sheep could be distinguished from a dog from a distance. "No," the rabbi simply answered. "When you can distinguish a pear tree from an apple tree?" a second chanced. "No" was the answer again. "When you can distinguish between a fox and a dog walking in front of you on the road." "No" yet again. "Please tell us the answer then," the rabbi's disciples pled. He answered, "When you can look into the face of another human being and have enough light to recognize him or her as your brother or sister, then you know that the night is ended, the darkness gone, and the light of the new day has arrived."

As Christians, Catholics live with the knowledge that the light *has* arrived, that with the advent of Jesus Christ the dawn from on high has broken and shines upon us, giving us light to guide our feet into the way of peace (Lk 1:78,79). We have the light, but often our vision is too weak to recognize the other as brother or sister. Service experiences situated in Catholic schools have as one important goal the development of dispositions among our students that allow them to recognize others as human persons made in the image and likeness of God. That is, one important area in which students should grow as a result of doing service is in the virtue of solidarity.

The *Catechism of the Catholic Church* defines a virtue as "an habitual and firm disposition" that "allows the person not only to perform good acts, but to give the best" of himself or herself (para. 1803). Virtues are neither innate nor infused. They are learned; they are, as the *Catechism* states, "acquired by human effort" (para. 1804).

What constitutes solidarity as a virtue? If prudence is defined as reason in action and justice as giving God and neighbor their due, how is solidarity defined? Pope John Paul II, who emphasized the disposition of solidarity as a virtue, described it in his encyclical *Sollicitudo Rei Socialis* (1987) as an awareness that as a result of the Incarnation of Jesus our brother, we are all sons and daughters of God, drawn together in unity as brothers and sisters by the life-giving action of the Holy Spirit. Additionally, solidarity includes the recognition of interdependence among individuals.

Solidarity is not a virtue esteemed by the world, however. Catholic school educators have multiple opportunities to participate in conversations with students about their experiences of serving. Imagine one such conversation in which a White upper-middle-class student mentions that among the things that he is learning from his experience of tutoring in a seventh-grade classroom at a school populated mostly by children from economically poor families of color is "to be more accepting." The language of tolerance he uses begs the question: What is he tolerating? The students? Their poverty? The structures maintaining inequalities between races and classes? The virtue of solidarity is not content with the discourse of tolerance; it requires a commitment to consider how one's condition is related to the condition of another.

Or imagine your puzzlement about an expression you repeatedly hear as you roam the hallways of your school: *o-b-k*. You know *l-o-l* means "laugh out loud" and that *b-t-w* means "by the way," but you cannot figure out what students mean when they refer to this or that student as "*o-b-k*." After weeks of hearing the expression, you finally muster the courage and ask a student to decode the letters for you, only to discover that they stand for "off brand kid," a student outcast (Erickson & O'Connor, 2000). Such an expression illustrates the American inclination to create lifestyle enclaves rather than community (Bellah, Madsen, Sullivan, Swindler, & Tipton, 1985) based in solidarity. The use of the term "off brand kid" underscores how consumerism and materialism inform the conduct of everyday life, including who are insiders and outsiders and how the resources of our culture are used to sort and rank people rather than to unite them.

Both of these illustrations emphasize the need for students to learn the virtue of solidarity, to learn to recognize the other as brother and sister and to learn a practical appreciation of the interdependence among people.

Learning the Virtue of Solidarity

As the *Catechism* makes clear, virtue is learned (paras. 1784, 1810). In this regard, learning to lead a virtuous life is not so different from learning artistic skills: Abstract, intellectual instruction is insufficient because virtues like art arise out of activity; to be learned, they require *practice*. Aristotle said so many years ago that we are what we do and that excellence is not so much an act as a habit. Contemporary learning theories help us to consider what it means for students to learn the virtue of solidarity in practice and how teaching can serve as an important resource for students' learning.

Helpful in this regard is the notion of the *zone of proximal development* (ZPD) of the Russian theorist Lev Vygotsky (d. 1934). Functions and abilities that have not yet developed are located in this developmental zone. Within the ZPD, students are afforded opportunities to internalize tools for thinking and acting in activities with the assistance of more capable others. In such a paradigm of moral development, growth in a virtuous life begins when a person internalizes the forms of activity associated with such a life (ways of thinking, feeling, acting). As Vygotsky notes, internalization occurs when external speech *between* people becomes inner speech *within* people (Tappan, 1998). In the Catholic tradition, we call this the education of conscience. Learning to lead a good life means learning the skills necessary for virtuous action.

As suggested in the story of the rabbi and his students recounted at the beginning of this chapter, the virtue of solidarity in particular requires skills of perception. Service programs are privileged places in this regard; they are opportunities for the "education of attention" (Ingold, 2000) of our students relative to the moral life. Properly structured service programs provide opportunities for students to learn both how those we first encounter as "other" are, in fact, brothers and sisters and how our lives our intertwined with one another. Tim Ingold, a British anthropologist, offers from his own life a helpful example about the assistance provided by a more capable other, his father, in coming to appreciate the flora of the countryside:

> When I was a child my father, who is a botanist, used to take me
> for walks in the countryside, pointing out on the way all the plants and

fungi – especially the fungi – that grew here and there. Sometimes he would get me to smell them, or to try out their distinctive tastes. His manner of teaching was to show me things, literally to point them out. If I would but notice the things to which he directed my attention, and recognise the sights, smells and tastes that he wanted me to experience because they were so dear to him, then I would discover for myself much of what he already knew. (2000, p. 20)

This provides some sense of an appropriate "pedagogy for solidarity" in service learning programs: The principal task of the more capable other is to point out, to direct the attention of students, to what matters. Ultimately, of course, the goal is for students themselves to learn both how to recognize and treat those they are serving as brothers and sisters and how to consider the ways in which their situations are interdependent.

In 1902 an Englishman by the name of Baron Friederich von Hugel was asked by a group of eager young Catholics at Oxford to address them. In the course of his talk, he referred to the person he regarded as the most extraordinary example of spiritual discipline in the previous century: Charles Darwin. Why Darwin? Why this person who in the previous decades had introduced such controversial theories? Because, he noted, Darwin had been willing to submit his wonderful intellectual powers and his great energy over a long period of time to the patient and painstaking observation of the development of barnacles, the shapes of finches' beaks, and all sorts of other details in nature (Himes, 1995). Living a good life requires taking the time to observe life and to reflect on experience in order to see what is *really* there. Not to see what one would like to be there or what one hopes is there or what one fears is there, but to see what is in fact there.

It is this sort of practice of disciplined reflection – among others – that service learning seeks to inculcate in our students. We want to help them learn how to take the necessary time to sift through all the images that are part of their interactions with others in service experiences in order to discern which ones are true and life-giving and which ones are illusions, which ones help them to see that the dawn has broken and which ones continue to obscure just how we are all children of God.

Recognizing Others as Brothers and Sisters

Service learning programs can help to inculcate in students a greater understanding both of "co-membership" with others and of the interdependence that exists among people.

Co-membership is defined as an aspect of social identity shared by persons in interaction (Erickson & Schultz, 1982). These shared aspects can include such things as race and ethnicity, gender, shared interest in hobbies, mutual friends, shared neighborhood, etc. When strangers meet, it is most often in the "small talk" of their encounter that they discover what it is they have in common, what aspects of their lives unite them. Finding these things held in common can take some amount of work; to discover commonalities that are possibly not initially apparent requires the ability to competently pursue social interaction with others. Ultimately, among the capabilities we expect students doing service in the Catholic context to learn are social skills that assist them to come to realize and appreciate their co-membership in the family of God with those whom they serve.

In his book *The Call of Service* (1993), Robert Coles recounts Catholic Worker Frank Donovan's story of Dorothy Day's dealing with a difficult guest at the Catholic Worker's house of hospitality in the Bowery. The guest was known for his fuming and ranting. One day Dorothy Day, a founder of the Catholic Worker movement, witnessed him glaring and cussing away, so she made a beeline to him and asked him about how he had found the soup that day. She then proceeded to offer her own critique of it, noting its bad taste was her fault because she was not such a good cook. In the course of her interaction with him, the guest calmed down. Those who witnessed the event came to realize just what was behind her words in the interaction with the guest:

> Maybe we are the only ones ready to feed you and listen to you, but we're in this mess called life *with* you. It's the *community*, we keep calling it, the *family*, all of us who break bread together, the way Jesus and His disciples did. (p. 243)

Serving without listening does not foster solidarity, a sense of community or family. How to listen at the service of solidarity is one very important skill to be learned in doing service.

The social skills necessary to find points of contact with another through social interaction are not innate; they are in fact learned. Learning to find such points, domains of co-membership, through attentive listening is a skill for which many students need the assistance of a more capable other. At soup kitchens, for instance, those who have such conversational skills (including more experienced students) can serve as models for newcomers by including them in conversations with guests. A follow-up discussion between the more capable veteran and the newcomer could provide an opportunity for the more skilled person to point out both the opportunities available in the interaction that fostered solidarity and what might have hampered such opportunities.

The example of the soup kitchen underscores the importance of having newcomer students working alongside more experienced people at service sites. Equally as important is the students' participation in their reflection on their experiences with more experienced people. Students' stories about their interactions with others provide opportunities similar to the ones Ingold's botanist father took advantage of during their walks together. That is, such stories about their service experiences can serve as occasions for more capable others to point out to things that matter, providing the students opportunities not only to make meaning of the experience but also to gain skills that foster a sense of community among those serving and being served.

Recognizing Interdependence

Solidarity has to do not only with the recognition of others as brothers and sisters but also with an awareness of our interdependence. The interdependence of members is a constitutive element of community and is among those things that distinguish a community from a lifestyle enclave (Bellah et al., 1985). It is for that reason that students' growth in awareness of the interdependence of people is an important learning goal for students involved in service. But solidarity goes beyond the simple recognition of interdependence because mere recognition of such interdependence does not rule out domination or exploitation. What is needed in addition to such an acknowledgement is a desire "to build the bonds of a common life" (Himes, 2001, p. 38). In this regard, a commitment to solidarity is closely connected to a commitment to the virtue of justice (discussed in the next chapter) for the dedication of people to solidarity encourages them to pursue "the good of all and of each individual, because we are all really responsible for all" (*Sollicitudo Rei Socialis*, para. 38).

Service programs designed for students to learn the tenets of Catholic social teaching benefit them by providing them with opportunities to consider such interdependence. For instance, students from suburban communities doing service in urban areas might consider how urban decline and suburban sprawl relate to one another. They might consider how suburban zoning laws prohibiting rental complexes and requiring larger parcels of land for houses ensure the concentration of lower income people in cities; how the expansion of housing in outlying areas demands greater spending on infra-structure like highways and sewers, draining resources from the existing city; and how the increase in property wealth in prosperous suburbs coupled with the decline in property wealth in the central city and contiguous, older suburbs means the transfer of a tax base from the poorest, most troubled communities to some of the most affluent, most prosperous ones (Orfield, 1997).

This example of urban sprawl as an intellectual focus in a particular sort of school-service context emphasizes the need for engaging in some sort of social analysis as a necessary part of the formation of Catholic youth in service. Engaging in social analysis serves as an appropriate corrective to the over-emphasis on therapeutic motivations for doing service. It suggests that an emotional commitment to regard others kindly is insufficient; growth in solidarity also requires an intellectual commitment to explore how the circumstances of humans are connected, how our lives implicate one another.

Conclusion

In his papal encyclical *Centesimus Annus* (1991) Pope John Paull II noted that in creating us God bestowed the divine image and likeness on us, conferring on us "an incomparable dignity" (para. 11). Assisting our students in Catholic schools and parishes in their growth in the practice of the virtue of solidarity provides them with a resource for their spiritual lives, with another means for them both to see that God's glory is, as St. Ireneus reminds us, the human person fully alive and to see the role they might play in giving glory to God by how they care for their brothers and sisters.

Discussion Questions

1. **Principle:** What ways of talking about service seem most likely to be successful in terms of understanding it as an experience of communion with Jesus?

2. **Strategy:** What ways can you ritualize "sending forth" students to service that will help students understand service in light of Matthew 25?

3. **Try tomorrow:** How would you respond to the student who states, "God helps those who help themselves"?

Resources

Bellah, R. N., Madsen, N., Sullivan, W. M., Swidler, A., & Tipton, S. M. (1985). *Habits of the heart: Individualism and commitment in American life.* Berkeley: CA: University of California Press.

Coles, R. (1993). *The call of service: A witness to idealism.* Boston: Houghton Mifflin Company.

Erickson, E., & Schultz, J. (1982). *The counselor as gatekeeper: Social interaction in interviews.* New York: Academic Press.

Erickson, J. A., & O'Connor, S. E. (2000). Service-learning: Does it promote or reduce prejudice? In C. O'Grady (Ed.), *Integrating service learning and multicultural education in colleges and universities* (pp. 59-70). Hillsdale, New Jersey: Lawrence Erlbaum Associates.

Himes, K. (2001). *Responses to 101 questions on Catholic social teaching.* Mahwah, NJ: Paulist Press.

Himes, M. (1995). Living conversation: Higher education in a Catholic context. *Conversations on Jesuit Higher Education, 8,* 21-27.

Ingold, T. (2000). *The perception of the environment: Essays on livelihood, dwelling and skill.* London: Routledge.

John Paul II. (1987) *Sollicitudo rei socialis: For the twentieth anniversary of Populorum Progressio*. Retrieved September 12, 2008, from http://www.vatican.va/holy_father/john_paul_ii/encyclicals/documents/hf_jp-ii_enc_30121987_sollicitudo-rei-socialis_en.html

John Paul II. (1991). *Centesimus annus: On the hundredth anniversary of Rerum Novarum*. Retrieved September 12, 2008, from http://www.vatican.va/holy_father/john_paul_ii/encyclicals/documents/hf_jp-ii_enc_01051991_centesimus-annus_en.html

Orfield, M. (1997). *Metropolitics: A regional agenda for community and stability*. Washington, DC: The Brookings Institution.

Tappan, M. B. (1998). Moral education in the zone of proximal development. *Journal of Moral Education, 27*, 141-160.

Chapter 3

Service as Charity/Service as Justice: How Justice Education Can Open Hearts, Inform Minds and Transform Students

Katie Murphy

I am convinced that service learning is transformative education. I came to this conclusion not because of education classes but as a result of my experience at Archbishop Carroll High School in Washington, DC. Since 1977, all students at Archbishop Carroll High School have participated in a social justice class that incorporates service learning. The late Robert Hoderny, a charismatic and committed teacher, began the program, and his class continues to change lives. When he died in 1996, I inherited the class with trepidation, but I came to realize that the power of the class came as much from the curriculum he created as from his passion and brilliance. My experience with this curriculum over the years has convinced me that service learning that weds charity with justice can be transformative.

This chapter considers service learning as a journey into charity and justice. It is the fruit not only of my twelve years of experimentation and reflection as a Catholic justice educator but also of my student's experience of service and reflection.

Anchoring Service in Prior Knowledge and Experience

Students do not begin service as blank slates; they begin with prior knowledge informed by their life experience. Our service learning focus is primarily on hunger and working at a soup kitchen. Consequently, we start our service learning with a reflection that attempts to uncover the students' feelings and thoughts (often stereotypes) about poor and homeless people in order to anchor the service in students' personal experiences. Students are assigned to write an "Autobiography on Hunger" in which they reflect on:

(1) hunger in their own life, (2) a significant experience with a hungry or homeless person, and (3) their expectations about the soup kitchen.

The students' reflections on hunger in their own life always surprise me. On its face, the purpose of this part of the reflection is for students to open their minds to what the clients at the soup kitchen might be feeling when they are served their food; the deeper goal is to open the hearts of our students to care.

Most students can relate to a time when they skipped a meal and their stomach hurt and how they felt irritable, tired, and distracted. Many students reflect on the extent of hunger's impact. Poignantly, some of our students have direct experience with hunger. Their reflections are powerful, deeply meaningful, and grace-filled. For instance, Brandon wrote about his realization that his father never ate with Brandon and his brother:

> I believe that my father never had enough money for us all to eat so he only focused on our well-being. After I came to this realization, I felt sadness because someone I knew and cared for went hungry while I was still eating. This makes me think twice about what I have and how much people have sacrificed to get it for me.

And Michael shared his experience of growing up in French Africa after his mother lost her job:

> I was just five years old. My brothers and I would walk at least 2 miles to carry water, in little plastic jugs. For as long as I can remember, the water was never clean. We would go for 2 or 3 days without water or food. We tried very hard to ignore the hunger with games. It was not long until we became homeless and hungry. My mother tried to make us feel as safe as possible by dividing us between her brothers and in-laws, but I still felt homeless. Later that month, my parents won the lottery, and we became one of the few families picked to come to the United States. We became the most privileged family in the entire world. We moved in on December of 2006; we were so happy because we now had shelter, clothing, food, clean water and other necessities.

Students like Brandon and Michael often become primary "soul educators" of the class. Sometimes, they ask me to read an excerpt of their essay anonymously. Other times, they tell their own story. And when the stories are shared, the class is changed.

Never in such circumstances has a student been made fun of; instead there is respectful silence after which another student usually raises his or her hand and says something affirming. Other students then speak up. The sharing unites us, and we become a community. Concern for their classmate often helps to change the vision of the students so that the next time they see a hungry or homeless person they feel and think differently than they had previously. Sharing personal experience plants seeds for transformative learning, while hearts begin to open and minds to wonder.

An important part of our work is uncovering stereotypes both in the personal reflections and in class discussions by encouraging students to share stories of significant personal experiences with homeless and hungry people. The responses vary dramatically from angry stories of hustlers and liars to happy stories of helping someone in need to sad stories of feeling unable to help. The challenge is to help students to recognize the impact of these experiences on their perception of the homeless and hungry and to open them up to a wider perspective. I try to achieve this by encouraging students to "bracket" judgments as they discuss their stories and impressions.

Different views are placed on the table, and we draw no conclusions. Because of the community-building work we have done, students generally feel safe enough to disagree with one another, to feel anger, and even at times to express dislike for the homeless or poor. The goal is for students to risk being vulnerable. The ensuing conversation is grace-filled as students help one another sort out the meaning of their experiences and attitudes. The next day in class, I have them write on an index card how they think their experiences affect their perspective on the poor and hungry. By the time their papers are due, the students have been pushed to reflect on their own attitudes and their origins.

In the final part of their "Autobiography on Hunger," students imagine what they think their service experience will be like. Before the paper is due, they write about their expectations of the soup kitchen on an index card that I return to them the next day with a question for further reflection. In this section, students often use convenient clichés that reveal a failure to think deeply, and I try to encourage a more analytic engagement with a prompt.

For example, to the students who write that it will be "fun," I ask why serving people who suffer would be fun. To the students who suggest that it will feel great, I ask why giving and sacrificing for others would feel great. How can giving (a "subtraction") become an "addition" spiritually in your life and another person's? What is God's math like? To students who expect that they will feel sad if they see a hungry baby, I ask how they think they could keep their heart open yet not become depressed. To students who are scared of the mentally ill, I encourage them to imagine how they might handle a challenging experience and what love might look like in that instance. My questions serve to help them to think personally, theologically, and philosophically.

Their final essays show realistic projection and introspection about the soup kitchen, while others demonstrate "soul-vision" and deep questioning about life. For instance, one student wrote that the soup kitchen "will feel like a 'happy grave' where the people feel happy they are getting a meal, but deep inside they are dying." This initial groundwork is crucial: Students' lenses become more focused, their minds more questioning, and hearts more open. Having had an opportunity to empathize with the hungry, uncover their assumptions, and project their hypotheses about their service experience, they are ready are serve.

Action: Service at the Soup Kitchen

I consider the actual experience of soup kitchen service as the most integral learning experience of the social justice class. In the first semester, all the students serve two times at the soup kitchen as a part of the class and are encouraged to serve one time on their own. My co-teachers, the school service coordinator, and soup kitchen staff guide the students' service experience; and I lead the class reflections.

On the assigned day of service, our service coordinator meets a group of students and orients them to the service experience. The service coordinator sets a friendly yet serious tone for the experience. They have been prepped in class and written their Autobiography on Hunger, and now is the time to act. They pray to see and experience Christ in their neighbors. As they make their way on the mini-bus to the soup kitchen, students are not allowed to use headphones – this is not a vacation from class but part of class. Science labs are places where our students experiment with test tubes; the soup kitchen is a sort of *religion* lab, where they experiment with Christian love.

Archbishop Carroll High School has been blessed with a forty-year relationship with a wonderful soup kitchen that loves our students. The soup kitchen staff, some of whom were themselves once homeless, take a special interest in the students and teach them more than how to cut carrots and make a meal. They talk with them and model how to show respect to guests. At the kitchen, the students rotate through different roles so that each has some direct contact with the homeless guests. Immediately after the service experience, the service coordinator assists the students in an initial reflection on the experience. The students fill out a "Discipleship Evaluation," a self-evaluation of their service; then the service coordinator evaluates their contribution. Our goal for them is to see themselves not simply as do-gooders, but as gooddoers and true disciples of Jesus.

The soup kitchen reflections are deeply personal and show emergent transformation. Shifts in perspectives and heart are evident; questions and thoughts about God, self, and neighbor abound. Consider the following excerpts from Jeffrey's and Luis's reflections:

I was consumed with my work and began to get drowned in the faces. I started to realize that no one in line was born as a stranger. Long ago that was someone's precious son or daughter, someone who was a loving member of a family. Each person had a story why they were there. Each person had a reason that they were in that situation, good or bad, their fault or not their fault. I then began to realize that my help was only temporary and was minimal at best. This made my work feel pointless. Then I realized when a man kept thanking me for his meal that what may seem useless to me, may mean a lot to them. (Jeffrey)

The soup kitchen became a doorway for me into reality. It allowed me to see beyond the life I have. It was a great experience and a memory that I will never forget. It has taught me that we, the people, must stand up for those who cannot stand up for themselves. We must become caretakers and accomplish the unbelievable. We must wipe out hunger. (Luis)

After an entire class has had an opportunity to serve at the soup kitchen, we have a class discussion. The discussion begins with a go-around during which each student shares a concrete reflection. I often give them a prompt with which to work: "When (*describe a vivid encounter*), I felt _____ because _____." I listen carefully and follow up with a question or discussion topic. I then try to be invisible, letting the discussion take on a life of its own. Students speak powerfully from their experience. For instance, last year a student saw a girl from her old neighborhood in line with her baby and *voom!* the entire class entered a deeper realm as they realized how poverty personally impacted them. Another great discussion followed some students' sharing their anger that they had been assigned to scrub the refrigerator instead of handing out plates to the hungry. This provoked other students to share their perspectives on what constitutes service. The bell usually rings too soon. Students are invested in the discussion and continue it as they exit the room.

After each time at the soup kitchen, I return their Discipleship Portfolios to the students, and they assess their learning in light of their Autobiography on Hunger, Soup Kitchen Essays, Discipleship Evaluation, and other class papers. I ask them to reflect on what they have learned about themselves, God, grace in the world, the hungry and homeless, society and justice. Service learning is a process, and continual self-evaluation deepens the learning.

Catholic Justice Curriculum

The focus on student learning distinguishes service-learning programs from service requirements. Service learning requires both teaching and a curriculum as resources for the learning. Within the context of a prayerful and sacramental Catholic community, our justice curriculum seeks to weave together the following elements: Catholic social teaching (CST), which draws upon revelation, reason, tradition, and experience (Massaro, 2000); critical analyses; examples of Christian witness; and justice activism opportunities.

Justice education begins with CST and seeks to incarnate our faith into the concrete circumstances of our everyday lives. In class, we investigate Christian love (charity) largely through reflection on the Bible. We prayerfully read the Bible to strengthen our knowledge and love of God's Word. We contrast the duty of Christian love that demands sacrifice and obliges us to serve our neighbor selflessly with the cheap, feel-good love promoted by secular culture. We study Jesus' witness and message of justice and the cost of discipleship. We also delve into the principles of CST. The philosopher Cornell West has said that "Justice is what love looks like in public"; the principles of CST paint a picture of public love for us. Justice affirms the dignity of the human person, demands that basic human rights are afforded to all, and works for the common good of all people and for the benefit of the earth. Justice seeks "the establishment of *shalom*, a community of peace where right relationships are restored" (Himes, 42).

Service learning prompts questions about life and about God, opening up the ground for a deep inquiry into their own faith. Students return to class from their service experience asking philosophical and theological questions about life, thus creating the perfect situation to crack open the Bible and reflect on Catholic doctrine. Because this inquiry is authentically rooted in their experience, it becomes something relevant, and students begin to formulate a worldview that incorporates principles of justice. For instance, when we reflect on "Lazarus and the Rich Man" (Lk 16:19-31), students see, feel, and hear the Gospel story differently after serving at the kitchen. The story becomes personal because they have met Lazarus. Concepts like human dignity and the preferential option for the poor are no longer abstract because the students have stories to tell about people whom they met. Service learning resembles an incarnation in this regard: Students begin in a new way to experience the truth and challenge of God's love as personal, present, and real.

The social analysis component of service-learning curricula in Catholic schools is crucial, for it enables us to step beyond conventional volunteerism to justice education. Service can *open* the heart to care, but justice education *informs* the heart and mind. It not only reinforces why students should serve others but also empowers them with the knowledge to work for justice.

Social analysis requires both a "bird's eye view" and an "on-the-ground view." Students are expected to know facts about hunger and homelessness and to demonstrate some skills in dissecting causes and imagining possible solutions. Besides the study of demographics and reports relative to the service situation, engaging guest speakers provide a richer understanding. We at Archbishop Carroll are partnered with the Capital Area Food Bank, an organization that presents an experiential workshop on hunger every year in our classes. We also are active with the National Alliance for the Homeless, and every year a homeless person shares his or her perspective. In class, we read articles and watch DVDs that help to personalize and show the human face of poverty. We want our students to care and know enough to act effectively on behalf of the most vulnerable in our society. Our students see the conditions of their hungry and homeless brothers and sisters and study the situation enough to make accurate judgments about the social conditions of the poor in our city. Then, they use the skills, knowledge, and sensibilities they have developed and write either a letter that calls for justice to an elected official or an editorial for possible publication in a local newspaper. The knowledge gained from class coupled with the authority gained from service results in powerful letters and editorials.

Such analysis of social issues not only enlightens the mind but also opens the heart to care. Often misinformation and stereotypes occlude the heart, stemming the flow of care; but considering the truth of a situation in the light of Catholic values can free a person to care. For instance, when students learned that the two largest groups of hungry in America are children and the elderly rather than drunks and addicts, they felt more open to the issue. In fact, in the self-evaluations of their moral journey in social justice, numerous students share that they grew in their care because they grew in their knowledge.

From Service as Charity to Service as Justice

Without the important work done in the classroom, it is difficult to move service learning from charity to justice. The danger of a service-learning curriculum without a justice strand is that the service could actually reinforce harmful stereotypes and legitimize unjust social structures. Service without attention to the demands of justice can lead to privileged students sharing food and clothes with their poorer neighbors in patronizing and demeaning means. Pope Benedict XVI captures this concern very well in his encyclical on Christian love: "Instead of contributing through individual works of charity to maintaining the status quo, we need to build a just social order in which all receive their share of the world's goods and no longer have to depend on charity" (*Deus Caritas Est*, para. 26). The pope's words echo words from the Second Vatican Council's *Decree on the Apostolate of the Laity*: "[T]he demands of justice [must first] be satisfied lest the giving of what is due in justice be represented as the offering of a charitable gift" (para. 8).

Knowledge of the "demands of justice" referred to by the Second Vatican Council is not innate; it is learned. Each year, I ask students to give examples of human rights. Inevitably, they mention civil rights like the freedom of speech and of religion; rarely do they mention economic rights and the right to food, clothing, shelter, and health care. When asked how they feel when they see a homeless person, they usually say that it makes them feel sad. In all my years of teaching the course not once has a student said that she felt angry that human rights were violated.

When I ask students to describe justice, they refer to punishment and the court system; they do not allude to the Christian conception of justice as the establishment of shalom as Himes (2001) describes. When they begin the justice course they are able both to recognize the homeless man and to want to feed him; what they are unable to do is see food as a human right.

The course acts as a resource for their learning; over the course of our time together, their vision sharpens and they begin to see how social policies like the low minimum wage, gentrification, and inadequate physical and mental health care give rise to homelessness. Putting justice and service together provides the students with stereoscopic lenses, allowing them to see clearly in order to make sound judgments leading to just actions on behalf of the most vulnerable of society.

Conclusion

Service learning that fosters charity for our neighbor and includes a well-planned justice component can empower students to step confidently out into the world and address complex situations. In a word, it is transformative. Repeatedly, I have witnessed such transformation in students. In that respect, the social justice course is a graced opportunity for students to change their minds, open their hearts, and strengthen their wills to do what is right for the least among us. And it all begins with the soup kitchen.

In an article about service, my mentor Robert Hoderny (1989) wrote, "Education has always been best when it sheds light on ignorance and sets people free to think critically. Can it not also set people free to care?" Without a doubt, service learning is Catholic education at its best because it informs the minds and opens the heart to live the Gospel. Service learning sets students free to love and change the world.

Recently, a student gave me an article ripped out of the paper. A shelter was being closed just as the nights were getting colder. Men whom we serve at our soup kitchen lived in that shelter. It was a call to action. We called a meeting of the school's Peace and Justice Club and discussed how to address the problem. The students were intense as they strategized about how they would approach the issue. After studying it further, they began to make calls to elected officials. I listened as they respectfully shared their informed opinion about the shelter's future. After club members composed an intelligent and proactive petition, they left my classroom armed with clipboards and determination. Their efforts resulted in a meeting with the council member from our ward.

As I watched my students hit the streets in their Catholic uniforms, the following words echoed in my heart:

He came to Nazareth, where he had grown up, and went according to his custom into the synagogue on the Sabbath day. He stood up to read and was handed a scroll of the prophet Isaiah. He unrolled the scroll and found the passage where it was written:

"The Spirit of the Lord is upon me, because he has anointed me to bring glad tidings to the poor.

He has sent me to proclaim liberty to captives and recovery of sight to the blind, to let the oppressed go free, and to proclaim a year acceptable to the Lord."

Rolling up the scroll, he handed it back to the attendant and sat down, and the eyes of all in the synagogue looked intently at him.

He said to them, "Today this scripture passage is fulfilled in your hearing." (Lk 4: 16-21)

And I thought to myself, "This is what Catholic education is all about."

*See Appendix A for a tool to assess students' disposition toward justice related concerns.

Discussion Questions

1. **Principle:** What ways of teaching students about the Catholic notions of justice seem the most likely to be successful?
2. **Strategy:** Can you think of activities you can provide to students in your school to help them understand how service, charity, and justice are related?
3. **Try tomorrow:** What specific social questions would you like your students to engage as part of their experience of service?

Resources

Hoderny, R. (1989, November). Setting them free to care. *Teacher magazine.* Downloaded on September 12, 2008, from http://www.teacher magazine.org/tm/articles/1989/11/01/2hoderny.h01.html?r=252063632

Pope Benedict XVI. (2005). *Deus caritas est.* Retrieved September 12, 2008, from http://www.vatican.va/holy_father/benedict_xvi/encyclicals/docu ments/hf_ben-xvi_enc_20051225_deus-caritas-est_en.html

Himes, K. R. (2001). *Responses to 101 questions on Catholic social teaching.* Mahwah, NJ: Paulist Press

Massaro, T. (2000). *Living justice: Catholic social teaching in action.* Lanham, MD: Rowman & Littlefiled.

Vatican Council II. (1965). *Decree on the apostolate of the laity.* Downloaded on September 12, 2008, from http://www.vatican.va/archive/hist_coun cils/ii_vatican_council/documents/vat-ii_decree_19651118_apostolicam -actuositatem_en.html

Chapter 4

The Works of Mercy: The Bedrock of Christian Service Learning Programs

James Skerl

> *The works of mercy are charitable actions by which we come to the aid of our neighbor in his spiritual and bodily necessities. Instructing, advising, consoling, comforting are spiritual works of mercy, as are forgiving and bearing wrongs patiently. The corporal works of mercy consist especially in feeding the hungry, sheltering the homeless, clothing the naked, visiting the sick and imprisoned, and burying the dead. (Catechism of the Catholic Church, para. 2447)*

One of the characteristics that mark high schools in the United States and most of the industrialized world, including Catholic high schools, is the "departmentalization" of knowledge according to subject disciplines (math, science, social sciences, fine arts, etc). The dangerous temptation is to treat the Christian formation of our youth in high schools as if it were like other subjects, to think that it, too, can somehow be divided into sections and domains. The problem with looking at formation in discipleship in this way is that such an approach can tend to overlook the integrity of the Christian life. For instance, for believers faith and justice are not experienced as separate, and neither are community and worship. I am convinced after thirty years spent forming the next generation in the Christian life that service and devotion should not be thought of as discrete aspects of the life of the believer but should instead be approached as different facets of a complete life of discipleship.

With the growing popularity of service programs in American schools, those of us teaching in Catholic schools can at times forget that for us service is rooted in discipleship. We scour mission statements and vision statements and program descriptions and pedagogical paradigms looking for help in articulating what service learning should look like in our schools. In fact, we only have to look to Jesus, who shows us how the works of mercy serve as life-giving encounters with him. In this chapter I present some of my reflections on how the works of mercy serve as the bedrock for an effective Christian service learning program.

Throughout the past forty years, Catholic religious education has undergone many developments. In the years following the Second Vatican Council, the winds of change pointed religious education in the direction of the affective domain rather than the cognitive. The result was an emphasis on the personal rather than the communal, on the spiritual rather than doctrinal, on the contemporary rather than the historical, on generic Christian spirituality rather than Catholicism grounded in Sacred Scripture and Tradition; on orthopraxis and social justice rather than orthodoxy and piety.

The 1992 publication of the *Catechism of the Catholic Church* served as a righteous rudder steadying the course of religious education, sparing it from being tossed and lost by shifts in currents. Because of the catechisms's influence, the direction of Catholic religious education has become clearer in recent years. Catholic religious education should not be framed as an "either/or" dichotomy but rather as a "both/and" vision, harmonizing both the mind and the heart; the communal and the personal; the doctrinal and the spiritual; the past and the present; right belief and right practice; and devotion and service. The place of our service programs can best be understood in this balanced, Catholic context.

Catholic education is relational in nature. Its purpose is to provide young people with the means to develop a personal relationship with God, in Jesus, through the Church. As a result, Catholic religious education has a three-fold function: to lead young people to *understand, experience,* and *practice* the Catholic faith. I am convinced that as part of a broader presentation of the faith a Christian service program should be relational and function within this three-fold framework of Catholic education.

Christian service programs in schools and parishes have emerged as integral parts of Catholic education. Even though the "hands-on" approach of a service program helps to give credibility to what is taught from the pulpit and in the classroom, service programs cannot take the place of a commitment to a solid *program* of catechesis. One effective way to integrate service with a broader catechetical plan uses the works of mercy as its operating system.

The Works of Mercy in the Life of the Church

We know from accounts in the Acts of the Apostles that the works of mercy have played a vital role in the life of the Church from its foundation. And the lives of holy men and women of every age marked by dedication to them (Francis of Assisi, Ignatius Loyola, Vincent de Paul, Martin de Porres, Teresa of Calcutta, for instance) have continued to energize the Church, reinvigorating it even in times of apathy, scandal, irrelevance, or crisis.

For young people, the works of mercy serve as a practicum in Catholic living, giving flesh to the Church's theology that students are introduced to in schools and parishes. They are truly catholic (in the original and fuller sense of the word, meaning "universal" and "open to all truth"): They are at the same time both ancient and new, traditional and contemporary, "old school" and cutting edge. Just as we have been assured that the poor will always be with us, we can be certain that the works of mercy will be needed in every age.

The works of mercy are most clearly presented in Chapter 25 of Matthew's Gospel. Jesus surprises us with the story of the Last Judgment (or should the story be entitled, "Mercy is as Mercy Does"?). Christ reveals that he comes to us in the most unexpected of ways. Shockingly, the Lord of Life identifies not with the greatest or the most powerful, but with the least among us. He appears in distressing disguise as beggar, as leper, as lonely, as guilty – as one with the least of God's people, our brothers and sisters.

It is hard not to notice just where this story of the Last Judgment in Matthew's gospel is placed. The words "Whatsoever you do to the least of my brothers and sisters…" are Jesus' last prior to the account of his passion. Any questions about whether Jesus actually meant what he said in the story of the Last Judgment are answered by his passion. In the passion, Jesus, the Son of God, literally becomes the least among us, the Suffering Servant. As we follow Jesus from the Upper Room to Gethsemane and then to Golgotha, we see that Jesus is the one who hungers and thirsts; he is the one who is abandoned by all, becoming a stranger; the one who is stripped naked of his clothes; the one who is sick with worry; the one who is shackled and beaten and thrown into prison, helpless at the hour of death; the one who is in need of burial. The spirit of Matthew 25 rings true: The least among us matters the most. The least among us is Jesus.

In feeding the hungry, giving drink to the thirsty, sheltering the homeless, clothing the naked, comforting the sick, and visiting the imprisoned, we are drawn into a relationship with Jesus, who is himself present in people who are neglected and rejected, destitute and lonely, forsaken and condemned. The corporal works of mercy are personal and communal responses to human suffering that have kept the faith alive throughout the ages and have been the social program of the Church for two millennia.

Jesus' story of divine mercy presents us with more than a simple outline for a social service program: we learn from Jesus in Matthew 25 that the works of mercy are authentic ways to encounter the living God. Love of God and love of neighbor are united in Jesus. It is out of this realization that we can speak of a "preferential option for the poor." Jesus teaches us the commutative property: communion with God leads us into to communion with others, and communion with others leads us into communion with God. When we learn to love others with compassion and consolation, we are learning to love as God loves.

The beauty of Matthew 25 is that it makes living the Gospel – as challenging as it is to live – accessible to us all. God's life-giving grace is not remote or distant. Rather, Jesus opens our eyes to see that this grace is as close as our brothers and sisters in need. Service done in love is the way *of* Jesus that simultaneously serves as the way *to* Jesus.

The Works of Mercy and Service Learning

As the works of mercy have transformed the Church down through the ages, they can do the same in the present age for a parish or school. The works of mercy are instrumental in building in our parishes, homes, schools, and communities a culture of grace and a civilization of love where the presence of God can be experienced and honored.

In his encyclical *Deus Caritas Est* (2005), Pope Benedict XVI reminds us to that the practice of charity (exemplified in the works of mercy) is no less important to the mission of the Church than the proclamation of the Word of God and the celebration of the Sacraments: "For the Church, charity is not a kind of welfare activity which could equally well be left to others, but is a part of her nature, an indispensable expression of her very being" (para. 25). A properly designed program of Christian service fulfills its role in our Catholic tradition when it brings together these holy activities that mark the Church.

I am convinced that we should be unapologetic and unabashed about the sacramental nature of our Christian service programs. To say that something is "sacramental," is to highlight its help in our experiencing the saving presence of God in our world. The works of mercy are sacramental: they are tangible, real ways of encountering the Lord. People who are poor, marginalized, ostracized, alien, rejected – all these and many more – come to know the God of mercy through people who live the works of mercy. And, as we have seen, those performing the works encounter the Lord in them. A work of mercy is a moment of communion.

Over ten years ago, I began a service opportunity that complements St. Ignatius High School's formal service-learning curriculum, which is centered on a one-semester, weekly, half-day commitment during the sophomore year at various sites within striking distance of our urban campus. This service opportunity is a ministry to the homeless and has as its patron St. Benedict Joseph Labre, who lived the life of a pilgrim, foregoing permanent housing and living solely on alms. Each Sunday afternoon students and their parents, faculty members and their families, and alumni of the school come to prepare food and pray together before setting out into the streets of Cleveland, Ohio, where we bring not only food but also friendship to the homeless poor.

When I began the project, I never imagined the impact it would have on our school community and on so many of our student and adult members. The Labre project has served as a sort of "school for the Christian life." This is due in large part, I think, to its basis in the devout life.

After we have made the sandwiches that we will share with our homeless neighbors, we head over to the school's St. Mary of the Assumption Chapel and gather before the Blessed Sacrament, where we pray quietly together in the presence of Jesus. This quiet time ends with a prayer to our patron, who had his own devotion to the Blessed Sacrament:

> Saint Benedict Joseph Labre, you gave up honor, money, and home for love of Jesus. Help us to set our hearts on Jesus and not on the things of this world. You lived in obscurity among the poor in the streets. Enable us to see Jesus in our poor brothers and sisters and not judge by appearances. Make us realize that in them we are helping Jesus. Show us how to befriend them and not pass them by.
>
> Saint Benedict Joseph Labre, you had a great love for prayer. Obtain for us the grace of persevering prayer, especially adoration of Jesus in the Most Blessed Sacrament.
>
> Saint Benedict Joseph Labre, poor in the eyes of people but rich in the eyes of God, pray for us. Amen.

In fact, this prayer is answered. God bestows immense graces, evident in the conversations among the participants as they talk about their developing friendships with our neighbors over the course of weeks. As one alumnus has put it, "Instead of fearing them, we try to dissolve the 'us and them' and create an 'us and us'" (Calloway, 2005, p. 44).

The Labre Ministry illustrates how service programs can make a genuine contribution to the formation in faith of students (and adults!) – their learning – when they foster a direct, sacramental connection between Christian service and the life of the Church. One way to envision service is as an extension of the Mass. Our self-offering for others in our service is done through Jesus, with Jesus, and in Jesus, in the unity of the Holy Spirit, to the glory of God the Father, and for the life of the world. The food and drink we give to the hungry and thirsty are signs of love. As such, they are extensions of the sacred food and drink that we share in the liturgy. "Go in peace to love and serve the Lord" are words that send us forth from the most holy communion to the holy communion of service.

We who are responsible for the Christian formation of our youth do them a great favor when we help them make this connection between Jesus' self-giving celebrated at the altar and the loving sacrifice of their service to others. We reverence Christ present in the action of the Eucharist and his abiding presence in the tabernacle; and, following Jesus' counsel in Matthew 25, we likewise reverence his presence in the least among us. Prayer before the

Blessed Sacrament as part of a service program is a quiet, profound way to help students in our Catholic schools and parishes to grow in their under-standing and appreciation of the sacramentality of their service.

Christocentric Service

Christ is the "content" of learning that distinguishes *Christian* service learning from other sorts. Whatever other legitimate matters might be pur-sued, those forming youth in Christian service always remain focused on helping young people grow in their relationship with Jesus Christ. Programs of faith formation should first invite participants into "the one thing neces-sary" (Lk 11:42): a relationship with God in Christ Jesus. Prayer and service should be connected. Opportunities to reflect both on their prayer and service, to articulate their religious experiences, are opportunities for our students to grow in their understanding of who God is, what God is about, and where God can be found. Such reflection has a vocational aspect, too, I have found: Students discover more clearly who they are, what they are to be about, and where they are to go.

Because the service we render as Catholic Christians is not simply about being nice, I think students in Christian service programs should be sent out to serve *in the name of Jesus*. My own experience suggests that ritualizing this "sending forth" in a footwashing ceremony, for instance, enables young people to experience themselves as disciples of the Lord commissioned to do his work in his Spirit. Such a ritual helps students come to a spiritual un-derstanding that identifies their service work with the work of Jesus. When do we know we have succeeded in helping them in this regard? When they are moved to say in whatever words, "Christ's work is my work."

I am advocating in this chapter for a service learning program that is Christocentric *by design*. In preaching, classes, and retreats, priests and dea-cons and campus ministers, directors of service, and teachers rightfully in-troduce young people to the teachings of Christ, the miracles of Christ, the prayers of Christ – even to the parables and paradox of Christ. Service pro-grams have a unique opportunity to further the Christocentric mission of Catholic education by challenging students to know Jesus in a new way: the Wounds of Christ.

Christ's wounds point to his humanity. He "emptied himself, taking the form of a slave," becoming "obedient to the point of death, even death on a cross" (Phil. 2:7-8). Through practicing the works of mercy, students are asked to pattern their lives on Jesus, who took on human suffering so as to transform it into an act of love. In learning to associate the pain of human suffering with the wounds of Christ, young people can come to a personal, felt knowledge of the passion, death, and resurrection of Jesus. The wounds by which we are saved (Is. 53:5) reveal God's unassailable love for us. If God is so merciful to us – shown in the life of self-offering of Jesus his only Son – what can we do in return for this "greatest" love? How do we celebrate God's victory in Jesus Christ over sin and death and division?

The works of mercy are opportunities for students to do the extraordinary: to touch the body of Christ. Just as for Thomas, seeing and touching the wounds of Christ is transformative. When Thomas touched the wounds of Jesus, there was no looking back: Doubting Thomas became Believing Thomas, Saint Thomas. Isn't this the hope we all have for the young people in our service programs? That in touching the wounds of Christ like Thomas they come personally to learn about God's deep and abiding love and so grow in their belief and desire to serve the Lord?

Christian service programs rooted in the works of mercy are bold initiatives. They are bold in what they seek to accomplish and bolder yet in what they ask of students. They ask young people to go beyond their current levels of comfort in order to offer comfort to others in their struggles and suffering. Service programs often ask students to go where they have never gone before – to places of pain and brokenness, even if one of those places is their own human heart.

We often think that people somehow know how to deal with pain and suffering naturally; in fact, I think knowing how to acknowledge one's own suffering, the suffering of others, and the suffering of the world is learned. And service is one privileged place for this learning to happen. One such opportunity for our students at St. Ignatius High School grew out of the Labre Ministry I mentioned above; we call it the Joseph of Arimathea Society.

St. Joseph of Arimathea is the patron for a group of students whose ministry is to bury the dead. These students serve as pallbearers at the funerals of homeless men and women or people who otherwise would have no one assisting at their funeral. In 1955 the Catholic author Flannery O'Connor published a short story entitled "You Can't Be any Poorer than Dead." That certainly is the realization of many of our students, who before serving in this ministry have never personally encountered death. The ministry brings them close to the ultimate pain and brokenness that makes no distinction among people. Whatever their own background, the students face the human condition common to us all. Our students learn that Jesus wants to meet us at those places where we are weakest, at the tombs of our lives.

In a culture that has devised so many ways to avoid all pain and suffering, it is quite strange and even counter-cultural to ask young people to go to such places, to seek out the wounds of Christ. Much of what service programs ask of students is contrary to modern cultural values. In selflessly living out the preferential option for the poor, students are being asked to do many things "contrary" to the values of the world: to befriend the unpopular, spend time with the powerless, even get to know the "un-pretty" and unclean, to care for the dead who cannot thank them. As Catholics, we believe that service is not optional, but instead, an integral part of our Catholic faith that our salvation depends on. Service programs formalize this gospel imperative for educational purposes, providing our students with opportunities, experiences, and perspectives the world cannot give.

Conclusion

Learning is transformative. Service learning programs rooted in the works of mercy offer students opportunities to learn skills of discipleship. More importantly such programs provide them an opportunity to develop a deep, personal relationship with Christ that will forever change them – and change their relationships with all whom they meet. As they encounter Jesus in the Eucharist, in the poor whom they serve, and in their personal prayer, they begin to develop a vision. They begin to see the world with the eyes of Jesus. They develop the spiritual resources not only of discipleship but also of apostleship, living as though the world were as Jesus envisions it in order to show the world what in fact it can be. They strive for the Kingdom of God.

Ultimately, of course, this is our goal as adults responsible for their formation in the Church. Adult leaders put so much time and effort and thought and prayer into the planning and implementation of Christian service-learning programs. We do this for many reasons, not the least of which is to invite students into full participation in the Church. We who have been charged with the care of their souls seek to serve our students well so that ultimately they themselves may one day hear the words from Matthew 25 spoken to the Saints: 'Come, you who are blessed by my Father. Inherit the kingdom prepared for you from the foundation of the world." It is a precious responsibility. Mercy is as mercy does.

Discussion Questions

1.   **Principle:** If service is rooted in discipleship, then how can schools develop service programs that teach to a complete life in discipleship? What are some elements programs require to impart this message?

2.   **Strategy:** When we serve people in direct and personal ways, we are drawn into a relationship with Jesus because he is in each per son we touch. What ways can service projects encourage students to pattern their lives on Jesus beyond the project activities and throughout the many facets of their lives?

3.   **Try tomorrow:** What angles of the "works of mercy" would ap peal most to your students and faculty? What angles will deepen their understanding and compassion toward their relationships with each other and the larger community?

Resources

Anderson, C. (2008). *A civilization of love: What every Catholic can do to transform the world*. New York: Harper One.

Calloway, T. (2005). Student profiles: Jodie Bowers, John Carroll University. *Conversations on Jesuit Higher Education, 28*, 44.

Keenan, J. F. (2005). *The works of mercy: The heart of Catholicism*. Lanham, MD: Rowan & Littlefield.

Pope Benedict XVI. (2005). *Deus caritas est*. Downloaded September 12, 2008 from www.vatican.va/holy_father/benedict_xvi/encyclicals/documents/hf_ben-xvi_enc_20051225_deus-caritas-est_en.html

United States Conference of Catholic Bishops. (2005). *National directory for catechesis*. Washington, DC.: United States Conference of Catholic Bishops.

Zwick, M. & Zwick, L. (2005). *The Catholic Worker movement: Intellectual and spiritual origins*. Mahwah, NJ: Paulist Press.

Chapter 5

Building Solidarity: How to See More Broadly and Engage More Deeply Through International Service Trips

Katherine Feely, SND

"You cannot step into the same river twice," asserted the Greek philosopher Heraclitus of Ephesus (c.535 BC - 475 BC). He pondered the dynamics of change and saw them as part of the innate workings of the universe. Heraclitus' statement is true on two essential levels. First, it is impossible to step twice into the same river because *the river* has flowed on; everything has changed. And second, not only has the river flowed on, but *the person* stepping into the river has flowed on too and has changed. This ancient wisdom of Heraclitus is true of service learning today. Young people cannot enter the stream of service and not be changed – changed by the nature of the experience and changed by the current of reflections and encounters they offer.

Service learning places students in the stream of life that by its very nature brings about a process of change and, with grace, leads to deeper conversion and apprehension of the gospel message. Done well, service learning offers a deepening of knowledge, a broadening of experience, and an encounter that can lead to personal, spiritual and social transformation. Service learning is an essential way to bring one's faith into contact with the real needs of the world. More and more, schools are exposing students to the real needs in countries beyond the borders of the United States. These border crossings offer tremendous opportunities to encounter another culture and require specific skills in helping students make sense of what they will encounter and how they engage.

This chapter explores three distinct considerations for international service trips, first, preparation and packing, second, pitfalls to avoid, and third, a pedagogy of global solidarity to support and strengthen the spiritual and educational opportunities afforded by such travel. Taken together, these tools can help service learning coordinators and teachers prepare well and help students navigate and make sense of their experience across borders and long after they return home.

Preparation & Packing

Preparation for a trip is not just about logistics and details but about the inner preparation needed to get ready for this type of experience. At the heart of the planning process the following three elements are essential if a service learning trip is to be about a deeper encounter and greater solidarity. These three elements include forming community, sustaining relationships and an ethic of care and responsibility upon return.

The first element required in the planning is to determine how you intend to form community both with those going and with those who will be met along the way. Forming strong community ties before hand will become a part of the witness value for all involved and move this from tourism to disciple based service.

The second essential element to consider in planning is how you intend to sustain the relationships fostered through the trip and what your commitment is to the longer term sustainability of the project. If you are building dependence on your generosity, or monetary donations, or even labor, what will happen when you no longer show up?

The third essential element you need to consider in the planning process is what you will do with your experience when you return home. How will you use your privilege and power to make a sustained effort at advocacy on behalf of those you served? What is your responsibility upon returning to honor the lives and dignity of those you encountered?

Unpacking

Before any packing should begin, the first thing that needs to happen is to explore the attitudes and motivations behind the trip along with the right and proper attitudes to bring along.

What to Unpack/Cultivate Before Embarking on a Service Trip

- Sensitivity to other cultures, respect and reverence.
- Awareness of the history, politics and economic conditions of the coun-

try you are serving – do your homework.

- Country literacy in current events: read the local newspaper of the country – read it online and if it's in another language use a free online translation service. Set up a "Google alert" about the place where you will be going.
- Sacrifice: connect fundraising for the receiving community to fundraising for the group going. The cost of the trip should not be more than the resources you provide for those you are serving. Look carefully at the ratio of money raised for your group to travel, vs. money raised for the people you are serving. If you aren't willing to raise as much or more for those you are going to serve this may be an indication telling you something about the real reason for the trip.
- Open hands, engaged hearts – be willing to go out of your comfort zone to be flexible and open, to reach out, to stay curious, to engage first and extend radical hospitality. Let go of any needs for control, attention or special consideration.

Trip Pitfalls to Avoid

- Don't go on a service learning trip to solve or fix problems; go to be present and listen deeply.
- Avoid the pitfall of raising money for your trip or your work by fostering pity or manipulating guilt. This does nothing to lift up the human dignity of the people with whom your students will be in relationship. Encourage generosity or sacrificial giving but avoid further victimizing others. This is a significant pitfall and one all too often at the heart of service learning trips.
- Avoid displays of first world consumption and over exuberance – too much food, too many photos, too much phone use. Students may need some clear expectations set so they don't embarrass themselves or others.
- Encourage solidarity in packing – have students learn about the socio economic level of the people they will be serving. Have them develop a list of what they think a person in that setting would have to use for the length of time they are there. Limit the numbers of pants/ shirts/jeans/so that they are also living at the level of those they are

serving – they experience what they take for granted, and have the opportunity to discover how little they truly need.

■ Where possible have students read an interesting historical novel, biography or first person account of someone (preferably close to their age) from the country they will be visiting. This is a great way to have them gain some insight and background knowledge before leaving. Get the English department involved in selecting or assigning such a book or developing a discussion guide.

■ Have students participate in setting clear ground rules before a trip. Set in the context of optimal communal well being, students will want to have a great experience and know well what can thwart that. Put students in charge of monitoring adherence to those rules and rotate that role.

■ The processing after the trip should be just as carefully done as the planning that preceded the trip. If you do three months of prep, plan on doing three months of processing after. This is often the most neglected aspect of service learning opportunities.

Pedagogy/Method for Global Solidarity

Solidarity is at the heart of the gospel and the Church's social teaching. It has vital implications for how one sees another and the world at large. Solidarity is that common bond of humanity that binds us to one another when we recognize that we are one human family. "Solidarity is the conviction that we are born into a fabric of relationships, that our humanity ties us to others, that the gospel consecrates those ties, and that the prophets tell us that those ties are the test by which our very holiness will be judged" (Fr. Bryan Hehir). There is no "us" and "them" there is only "we." This process can be used while engaged in the service learning experience or it can be used upon return to unravel and process the experience. A little bit of both is recommended.

Before launching into the descriptive nature of this section, first it is important to note that this methodology was formulated and emerged as a result of interviewing numerous teachers who had participated in the ***Frontiers of Justice*** program sponsored by NCEA and CRS. Teachers traveled to developing countries and learned about the lives and realities of others. One striking insight that was consistently expressed in the interview was the admission that these teachers did not totally grasp the ***principle*** of solidarity, until they had an actual ***experience*** of solidarity.

Over and over again, teachers identified how their experience transformed their understanding. In trying to understand solidarity, then, experience *was* indeed the best teacher. With that in mind what follows below is an attempt to offer a pedagogy of experience (for solidarity) with the hopes that teachers can find creative ways to engage and apply the educational process surrounding the service learning experience, in order to bring about the comprehension, transformation and education we all hope for.

Step One: Learning from Experience

Experiential service learning trips provide students with a priceless opportunity and a powerful tool far beyond the classroom. This kind of experience exposes students to vastly different places, foods, cultures, different socio-economic realties, and different ways of viewing life. They gain a different sense of others and themselves when they encounter what it means to live on the edge of literacy, society, poverty or survival. Understanding solidarity is easiest when it begins with an actual experience of solidarity.

Step Two: Reflecting on what is Happening

Encourage students to unravel and reflect on their experience. Too frequently in today's fast-paced world, students are over scheduled, over programmed, and prone to rush through one activity in order to race to the next activity, leaving little if any time for true reflection or integration to take place. This creates a condition I call 'perpetual motion indigestion'. Help students cultivate the art of exploring their experience and pealing away the layers of meaning. Help them to surface and savor the process of reflection and the search for meaning and deeper insight.

Engage follow up questions, and encourage students to identify:

1. Feelings
2. Insights
3. Places of disorientation and reorientation
4. Disturbances
5. Questions that emerged

Step Three: Grappling with the Context and the Causes

Challenge your students to identify the root causes of the context with which they find themselves confronted. Build on their prior knowledge and have them make connections to what they have already learned in their courses including world history, English, biology, etc. Create an educational dialogue between the experience, the context, and the content. When students return continue to weave in connections to the experience, which anchors and reinforces what they have learned. Consider having students work together to prepare integration projects (for example a PowerPoint presentation with photos, reflections, descriptions of what they will do with the experience to make a difference now that they are back, etc.) to present to their peers and parents.

Step Four: Engaging Analysis

Develop the critical thinking skills of your students in order to help them actually analyze the bigger picture. In this way, critical thinking becomes a natural part of their learning process. In any given setting, there are numerous assumptions and perceptions that are functioning both above and below the surface of things. Students are shaped and influenced by their family background and upbringing, as we all are. They are often unaware of the power this source of influence has on them or their worldview until it is brought out into the open for closer examination. Some elements of this analysis might include:

- *Naming Assumptions and Perceptions*
  Students often lack the awareness that they are operating out of a set of assumptions. By challenging them to identify their assumptions, they must first struggle to figure them out and then name them.
- *Analyzing Perspectives*
  When students can identify different perspectives and see an issue from various points of reference, they can begin to understand the complexities of situations and move beyond wholesale acceptance of only one view. They can surface different questions and cultivate different insights.
- *Identifying Power and its Uses*
  Every human being has circles of power and influence; these can be

either used positively, negatively, or neutrally. But the question to focus on for analysis is, "How is that power being used? Other questions to consider include: "What different kinds of power are active in the specific situation," "Who holds the power, and who lacks power?" and "Who is affected by the use of power, and how?"

Step Five: Bringing God into the Picture

Invite students to discuss ways they see God present in the reality, experience, or situation. Bring the light of scripture to bear on the topic. Look for connections to biblical figures who found themselves faced with similar circumstances or share similar themes. The human condition and the "problems" faced are ever ancient and ever new.

1. Look to the psalms of lament to see how the Israelites struggled with oppression, or greed, or slavery, or war.
2. Have students read the gospels to bring the teachings of Christ to the topic.
3. Lift up examples from church history that display similarities.
4. Discuss the outcomes.
5. Explore ways the Catholic Church is currently responding to various realties through individuals, faith communities, its social and charitable institutions, its advocacy networks and initiatives, its resources, and its global presence and influence.
6. And at every step along the way, encourage students to pray.

Step Six: Engaging in Action and Advocacy

True education does not merely impart information but rather transforms, bringing about personal and societal transformation. Understanding connections to one's faith is a good starting point, but true education must lead to putting faith in action at the service of others. Students must not only be aware of the demands of discipleship, they must put them in action.

After a service learning trip, students should come back home with more than photos or funny hats. They should come home with a plan and a strategy to put their experience to work. They can do this in a number of ways. One is to educate others. Tell the stories, show the pictures, but educate about what need to be done through channels of influence. Second, students should be encouraged to think through advocacy efforts that they can undertake as a result of their first-hand experience. Third, students should continue to learn about the systems of exclusion and oppression that make their service trip necessary in the first place and actively work to promote awareness and press for change.

Pedagogy of Global Solidarity for Service Learning Immersion Trips
(adapted)

1. Experience
Begin with experience and take time to fully enter into the service opportunity. Be present and mindful to what is happening.

2. Reflection
Reflect on experience & allow time to unravel the impact. Journaling is an essential tool and service journals are a good idea. Note thoughts and feelings, questions that are emerging.

3. Context & Content
Discuss the cultural realities, explore the historical, political and religious context of your setting making connections to prior knowledge or previous preparation. Connect it.

4. Analysis
Explore the ways that the experience is connected to power, economic system. Explore change in thinking and assumptions –the development of a broader outlook and awareness. Challenge students beyond reactions to analysis.

5. God in the Picture
Bring God into the picture and reflect on ways that God is present. Break open the scriptures and listen deeply to what is happening in the heart. Take the experience to prayer. Pray the experience together.

6. Engagement
Help students listen carefully to the actual and articulated needs of the people they are in relationship with so that when they return home they return with a responsibility to engage in advocacy in an informed and knowledgeable way.

Conclusion

The highest purpose of an education is not simply to make a living, but to shape a life destined for eternity. Service learning is a rich avenue to help students navigate a significant journey across borders, boundaries and new terrain. In the process, it is hoped that they will begin to discover their true selves, their deepest aspirations, their common humanity and a profound gratitude for simple joys. To see solutions when there appear to be none requires faith. To find resolutions in the midst of great human suffering requires hope. To see and respond to those in need as brothers and sisters requires solidarity. Faith must be brought to bear on each and every situation that confronts us. And through a deeper understanding and appreciation of the world, one's faith becomes a life-giving stream that leaves students forever changed.

Discussion Questions

1. **Principle:** Look at the *Pedagogy of Global Solidarity for Service Learning Immersion Trips* on page 56 and consider (1) the principle of each step and (2) how each step would manifest itself in your school's service learning preparation and post-trip processes.

2. **Strategy:** In preparing for an overseas trip, what questions might students wrestle with in advance to open their minds and hearts to the learning experience ahead of them?

3. **Try Tomorrow:** If human beings cannot step into the same river twice, what indicators, self-assessments and/or reflections would suggest meaningful and transformative personal change? If none are apparent, what action steps could the program take to heighten student self-awareness during the life-cycle of the service learning immersion trip?

Chapter 6

Lessons Along the Road to Emmaus: Helping Students Realize a Lifelong Vocation to Live in Service to Others

JoEllen Windau Cattapan

The story of two disciples traveling along the road to Emmaus (Lk 24:13-35) is an Easter favorite. We not only hear how Jesus surprises the two men after his death and resurrection, but we also are reminded of our own call to continue the mission of Jesus.

This story is especially important for men and women entering adulthood. This well-documented stage of life, known as the "quarter-life crisis," challenges men and women in their twenties as they begin to navigate and make sense of the many choices and responsibilities they face as they enter adulthood. The feelings of the two disciples depicted in the Gospel story as they set out on their journey after the loss of their teacher captures some of the same feelings men and women have as they travel along the road to personal maturity – sadness, confusion, and fear. Like the disciples in the story, young adults need the support and guidance of the community – and even of strangers! – along their journeys.

In my work with college-aged students and young adults in their 20s, I have noticed that those who have regularly participated in community service share something in common: a budding wisdom which sets them apart from their peers. They more readily take responsibility for their actions; they go out of their way to help others; and although some might have serious questions and concerns about their faith, they are steadfast seekers. They try to reconcile how their personal dreams and ambitions fit in with the needs of the community and what God is calling them to do. In this chapter, I hope to share with you the stories of how community service formed the sense of personal vocation among a few young adult men and women.

Relationships with mentors and teachers play an important role relative to service learning and the faith lives and sense of personal sense of vocation among students. The importance of such relationships is clear as the young adults I meet speak enthusiastically about such relationships. Without the relationships with mentors formed during service activities during high school years and beyond, the young adults I have worked with would not have ended up pursuing lives devoted to service. In what follows, I hope to illustrate in particular two important things for vocational discovery that young adults can learn from their relationships with teachers and mentors in service learning programs: (1) the importance of remaining open to possibilities; and (2) the importance of appreciating their faith as a foundation for making personal decisions.

Open to Possibilities

The two disciples encountered a stranger along the way to Emmaus. Instead of passing him by, they engaged in conversation with this man, sharing their sorrow over the loss of Jesus and enjoying the companionship of this stranger. They even urged him to stay with them instead of continuing on: "Stay with us, for it is nearly evening and the day is almost over." (Lk 24:28). They were open to what this new friendship might bring them. And what blessings did come! When Jesus took the bread and broke it, they realized their longtime friend and teacher was always with them.

An age such as ours, filled as it is with endless choices and opportunities, makes discernment and the discovery of life's purpose and vocation particularly difficult. The options available to men and women who are embarking upon the life stage of independence and self-sufficiency can be overwhelming. The constant temptation for many is to cope with the multitude of possibilities for their future by quickly closing off as many as possible. Additionally, our obsession with personal success can skew expectations, stop people from following a path that seems uncertain, and discourage them from taking a risk. Many of the young adults with whom I work do not dwell upon what they don't have or what they ultimately want out of life. Instead, they actively engage the present and take advantage of the opportunities that come their way. For many of these young adults it is the relationships with their mentors and teachers in service programs that taught them to be open to the possibilities of life, to be like the disciples who realized the blessings of the moment, of chance encounters.

A Life Changing Phone Call

I think of Adam Dufault, for instance. During his undergraduate years, Adam was a student in the School of Foreign Service (SFS) at Georgetown University. Legendary for its rigorous curriculum of economics, politics, and language requirements, the SFS demands intense study and commitment. As Adam imagined the career trajectory his studies were preparing him for, he was dissatisfied and uninspired. He found himself recalling relationships he had built with the campus ministers, theology teachers, and others involved with the service program at his high school. Although he did not realize it at the time, they had shown him an alternative possibility for his future. "They were the first adults who talked about the deep meaning of what they did. They talked about the personal investment in their work. And they talked about why they made the choices they did and why they worked in high schools and campus ministry."

The influence of mentors did not stop in high school. Adam was a work-study student for a woman who coordinated the peace and justice activities at Georgetown. Part of his job was to help the director with a project that supported recent graduates doing a year or two of service after college. While working on this project during his senior year, his calling came in a literal sense. "I got a phone call from volunteer program in Chicago. I don't know how they found my number and name. The guy called me and talked to me about volunteering with St. Procopius School." Adam, recalling one of the young alumni volunteers he had met in the course of his work-study duties and how "alive" she was, made the commitment to serve at St. Procopius. "I really thought it was going to be a one-year thing. I have been at the school for seven years now. I don't think I would have been open to service if I would have only done the SFS track at Georgetown," Adam notes.

Adam's high school involvement in campus ministry and service and his relationships with his mentors served as resources for his discernment, helping him to judge the different possibilities before him and giving him the courage to make a change that ultimately led him to his vocation. After volunteering for two years, he became a teacher and got his teaching credential. Adam is now the principal at St. Procopius School.

A Broader Worldview

Sarah Kilibarda is another young adult who was open to possibilities. When Sarah was in high school at Cretin-Derham Hall in St. Paul, Minnesota, she had two teachers who taught a class that combined English, economics, and religion with community service. "As a high school student, I felt like I was sheltered until that class," Sarah explains. "The teachers really opened my eyes to different experiences. Literature. We read a lot, but not the classics." Instead, they read books like *There Are No Children Here* by Alex Kotlowitz. Through that class, she learned that other peoples' lives are very different from her own, and she was motivated to do the unusual and pursue a life of service.

Sarah remembers how she wanted to do a year of volunteer service immediately following her high school graduation. Her parents convinced her to attend college first, but she was able to follow up her high school service experiences with volunteering and service trips during college. After college, she volunteered with Catholic Charities of the Archdiocese of Dallas. She did not know what she wanted to do in life, but her work as a counselor in immigration services began to open her eyes to possibilities. As a result of her work, Sarah met immigration attorneys and saw what they did; she became very interested in their work and began thinking about legal advocacy as service. Today Sarah is an immigration lawyer at a firm in the Twin Cities. *And* she is still open to possibilities: "My clients influence me in different ways. I am getting a broader worldview through them."

A Realized Capacity to Care

Kevin Nuechterlein is a sophomore at Loyola University Chicago. Although his own vocational journey is just beginning, he is making choices and building relationships with others that will encourage him to stay open to possibilities. When Kevin talks about his gifts and skills, he mentions his ability to make people feel at home and welcomed. During high school, Kevin participated in a service trip to the Dominican Republic, where he lived with a host family. "The hospitality of the family totally blew me away. It was amazing. It gave me strength during my time in totally different surroundings," he notes. At school, Kevin returns the gift of hospitality that he experienced by participating in a companioning program that helps first-year students transition to college. "We help the freshmen and are mentors to them. I can share my experiences of college, and hopefully that will help them in their transitions," Kevin explains. He is putting his gifts realized in a service experience to work for the good of others.

Remaining open to possibilities in life is a risky venture and hard to do without the help of others. Adam had the support of his mentors; Sarah had her teachers to show her the differences found in the world, and Kevin had the warm hospitality of his host family to make him feel comfortable when in another country. All three of these young adults have been blessed with mentors and models during their service opportunities, and these relationships helped to form their vocational choices.

A Foundation for the Future

The road to Emmaus was a rich journey for the two disciples. After they became aware of Jesus' presence, they recognized the familiarity of his message: "Were not our hearts burning while he spoke on the way and opened the scriptures to us?" (Lk 24:32). Jesus prepared his disciples for how they should live their lives with an understanding and knowledge of the scriptures. Although not physically present, Jesus would always be in their midst. He had given his followers the foundation for continuing his mission.

Making life decisions is not easy. A foundation is necessary in order to discern what is best for one's future. As Christians, we believe our faith is that foundation. But how best can we share our faith in today's culture? Direct instruction does not appeal to generations accustomed to more active engagement, more hands-on learning. Our students are looking for experiences of service that make their faith come alive.

Jeff Kaster (2008), director of the Youth in Theology and Ministry program at St. John's School of Theology in Minnesota, believes that Christian formation programs that integrate religious education, service, prayer, and vocational discernment within a community of peers are the most successful at fostering significant Christian discipleship. The young adults with whom I interact confirm Kaster's (2008) position. Only when service is situated in a larger context that provides opportunities for reflection with mentors, educators, and peers do the principles of our faith come alive for them. More importantly, the relevance of these values remains with them through the memories of their interactions and relationships with others.

Be Imitators of Christ

Jessica Melton, a high school alumna with community service hours totaling far more than those required for graduation, knows first hand how the foundation of faith is vital for teaching personal responsibility. For several years after college, Jessica taught English to junior and senior high schools students at a non-religiously affiliated private school in Washington, DC. When situations arose that required her to teach the students about personal responsibility, she found it difficult to do so without reference to a moral foundation like the one she had from her faith. Such moments would often cause her to think back to how her own formation served as a resource for living a virtuous life.

Jessica attended Notre Dame Catholic High School in Fairfield, Connecticut, where students had numerous opportunities both for community service and for building significant relationships with teachers outside the classroom. "I had uniquely dedicated teachers who poured themselves into the clubs I worked with. They modeled service for the students. It never felt like they were doing this work because they had to. They did it because they liked it," Jessica explained.

The Appalachia Club was one of Jessica's favorite community service projects. "Fr. Larry Carroll, one of the chaplains at the school, had an ability to help us recall the memories of the trip throughout the year. He made it so real for us," Jessica recalls. He also integrated the school's motto – "Be imitators of Christ" – into discussions about the trip. Jessica's understanding of Christian discipleship first developed during high school. "My high school experience didn't just influence it. It helped to define it... I didn't have to wonder if I was a disciple of Christ. We talked about it. We really examined service's fit with the mission of the school," Jessica explains. "I feel like I have a responsibility. This is who we are as human beings. As followers of Christ, we are supposed to do this service," she adds.

During college, Jessica thought she would pursue a law degree and politics, but her work with campus residence life during and after college opened other vistas for her. She went into teaching instead. "I have to have a human face to what I am doing. Politics and service could never be the same for me. I need to know the people I am serving." Today Jessica is in graduate school studying international education development at the University of Pennsylvania.

Championing Human Dignity

Katie Cranor is a graduate student in pastoral studies at Loyola University Chicago. For her, the seeds for pursuing a life of service were planted during high school. Katie attended a public high school, so it was parish-based mentors and their faith-filled commitment to others who played a particularly important role in planting and nurturing these seeds. Through the example of three women mentors in particular, she learned some valuable lessons about the dignity of people. As Katie explains, "They collectively influenced me in choosing career paths that are valuable to the health and well-being of society. They lived out of their values, even when it was uncomfortable. They modeled behavior. Their leadership and the inclusion of their faith in their actions was profound and inspiring."

Katie remembers as an instance of such leadership a time when racial tensions were high at her puplic high school in Rochester, Minnesota. One parish mentor, Jean Martin, was at the time an employee at the local victims services offices. (She later became the organization's executive director.) "We had violence," Katie recalls. "Jean recognized this violence and knew that raising awareness and education could help resolve some of the tensions. She started a program in the high school and facilitated it for high school leaders." Katie was one of the high school leaders who participated in the training, and she learned a valuable lesson from this experience. "When we function as a community, we are always better. We are always greater than the sum of our parts. Jean Martin's desire to develop the violence awareness program at my high school taught me this," Katie remembers. "Without her intervention, the violence would have continued in our high school. She did this on her own time. It was not part of her job description. She saw a need."

In Katie's subsequent volunteer activities throughout college and during a year of service with the Jesuit Volunteer Corps in Alaska, her commitment to honoring the dignity of people continued to develop. "It is extremely valuable to be immersed in the communities that are different from those what we know, but we always have to recognize and respect the people we are serving. So many times when service is done, there is no education on the history of the area. For instance, why is the city of Chicago divided between the North Side and the South Side? We need to have open dialogue between the people who are serving and those being served about what the needs really are. And those of us serving need to be open to hearing 'We don't want you'."

Katie's experiences of service and the example of mentors have prepared her for her present work as a graduate intern in University Ministry at Loyola University Chicago. As a mentor to a group of students who volunteer weekly, Katie finds herself in a position to challenge their perceptions and attitudes. She wants them to think about and question what kind of impact they are having on the people and communities they serve.

Both Jessica and Katie embody values of the Catholic tradition thanks in large part to teachers and mentors they met during their high school careers. Jessica realizes how difficult conversations about personal responsibility and what we owe to others in community are without a foundation in faith. Her own background and the mentors in her life have provided her with a knowledge and language to talk about such responsibility. Katie is a champion of the social teaching found within the Catholic tradition. Her desire to champion the dignity of the human person is inspiring and came from inspirational mentors.

Conclusion

These five young adults are pursuing lives of service in large part because of their involvement in high school community service programs and the relationships with key mentors associated with them. There are many more young people like them. And this should give all those involved with the

Christian formation of our youth cause for celebration and should encourage them to continue their commitment to making community service an integral part of the education of teens. These young adults not only learned to stay open to possibilities, to discern choices, and to develop an appreciation for their faith as a foundation for their lives, but they also learned the value of personal interaction and relationships.

Even those students who do not enter a "service profession" are positively impacted by the relationships with teachers and mentors in high schools whom they meet in the course of serving. What they learn in serving and what they learn from the adults who encourage and support their service and reflection provide them with gifts and skills that benefit society and serve the common good.

The old saying goes, "The proof of the pudding is in the eating." These stories of alumni of service programs at Catholic high schools and parishes suggest that any evaluation of a service learning program's effectiveness should include the input of alumni. One useful tool in this regard might be the use of a scale to measure Christian discipleship like the one developed by Jeff Kaster (2008). Using such a measure along with interviews of young adult alumni can help schools and parishes to identify areas of success and improvement relative to the formation of Christian disciples.

Having realized Jesus Christ in their midst in the breaking of the bread, the disciples on the road to Emmaus came to understand that there was more to the story than they had imagined. The encounter with Jesus meant seeing him differently – but also seeing themselves in a new way. Cardinal Bernadin, the late archbishop of Chicago, once preached that the two disciples realized that they were "not ex-followers of a dead prophet, but disciples of the risen Lord." The encounter with Jesus warmed their hearts, opened their eyes, and they were moved to share their experience with others. We want nothing less for our students.

Discussion Questions

1. **Principle:** How is service articulated in light of your school's mission? What opportunities do your students have to hear adults in the school talk about their own vocations to serve?

2. **Strategy:** How can you learn about the lasting affects of service learning in the ongoing lives of graduates? How can what you learn make a difference?

3. **Try tomorrow:** What is one specific way you could convey a stance that reveals an openness to possibilities as part of the disposition of a disciple?

Resources

Billig, S. H. (2000). Research on school-based service learning: The evidence builds. *Phi Delta Kappan, 81*, 658-664.

Kaster, J. J. (2008). *Assessing Christian discipleship formation in Catholic youth ministry*. Unpublished doctoral dissertation, University of Minnesota, Minneapolis, MN.

Chapter 7

Protesting Injustice to Demonstrate God's Love

Christian Tomsey

Of all forms of education, those activities that take us and our students beyond the four walls of the classroom seem to have the greatest potential for lasting impact. Perhaps it is the departure from the "usual" learning experience; perhaps it is the transformative act of a journey in itself; perhaps it is the sense of accomplishing something in the greater world – perhaps it is a combination of these things. Whatever the reasons may be, we often find that organized, external experiences live longest in the hearts of our students. Educationally, this seems to be the crux of service learning: moving students into the wider world, exposing them to the lives of others, and encouraging them to take action. In short, we ask our students to look, judge, and act.

Journeys and demonstrations of protest – though passive in a certain sense – serve as a vital gateway to greater and more active service in a world that yearns for the intervention of the young in the evils of the old. Moreover, organized participation in protests is relatively safe for student groups and provides ample opportunity for discussion and reflection without the burden of having to teach new skills. This realization has been a journey in and of itself for me as an educator and is a turning point that I think important to share with others.

Protesting What?

When I was asked to help lead a group of my high school students from Whitefish Bay, Wisconsin, to Washington, DC to participate in the annual March for Life, I wasn't entirely certain how I felt. The pro-life position and its attendant activities have increasingly been used as a platform for agendas which seem in some ways contrary to the cause; furthermore, cherished ideas about life have become conflated and muddied in the hands and mouths of politicians and orators. Why, I thought, don't we march for *all* life? After all, the Second Vatican Council made clear in *Gaudium et Spes*, the pastoral constitution on the Church in the modern world, that the Church is concerned with any injustice that threatens human dignity:

> [W]hatever is opposed to life itself, such as any type of murder, genocide, abortion, euthanasia or willful self-destruction, whatever violates the integrity of the human person, such as mutilation, torments inflicted on body or mind, attempts to coerce the will itself; whatever insults human dignity, such as subhuman living conditions, arbitrary imprisonment, deportation, slavery, prostitution, the selling of women and children; as well as disgraceful working conditions, where men are treated as mere tools for profit, rather than as free and responsible persons; all these things and others of their like are infamies indeed. (para. 72)

Where are the marches for the victims of these horrors listed by the bishops at Vatican II?

These were not the only misgivings I was encountering as we boarded the bus. A nagging thought had been following me since the moment I agreed to go along: What exactly is the point of a protest? I'd been asking myself this question since my own high school years when our school's Amnesty International chapter staged an anti-apartheid letter-writing campaign. What, I asked myself and anyone who would listen, will *that* change? Did protests stop the war in Vietnam or end systemic racism in our own nation? Have they yet made even one inch of progress against the horror of abortion?

I was questioning not the value of protest but rather the sufficiency of the reasons given for high schools to make time for their students to engage in the activity. I wondered whether my own students' time might not be better spent reproducing and distributing educational literature or volunteering at an area shelter, a counseling center, or office? Why spend time demonstrating when so much "active" or "direct" work remains to be done?

As I pondered these things, our motor coach rumbled down the Ohio Turnpike, holding boys and girls of diverse backgrounds but unified ideals. Dominican High School students left Whitefish Bay to help redefine what it means to be pro-life. They set out to speak against *Roe v. Wade* to be certain, but they also wanted to stand against callous treatment of all human life in all regards. I witnessed their growing convictions and found myself wondering: Would their voices be heard?

The plan they had brought forth was not a simple refutation of abortion. It was a consistent ethic of life, a call for the celebration and defense of all life. We were going to DC not only to participate in the March for Life but also to bear witness to the horrors of the Nazi Holocaust. We were going to the National Mall not only to remember the innocents killed because of abortion but also to read the names on the Vietnam Veterans Memorial Wall, to see the terrified faces of the soldiers at the Korean War Memorial, and to bear witness to the thousands of tombstones, row on row, that make up Arlington National Cemetery. We were going, by the students' design and the adults' gentle direction, to pause and reflect on what life means "from womb to tomb." These additions to our mission were made not at the request of our principal or our campus minister but at the insistence of our "Lifers," a group of students whose chosen moniker suggests their long-term commitment to all life. As freshman Allie reflected, "I wish the term Pro-Life was less one-dimensional. I noticed a 'Save Darfur' sign. A lot of people say they're pro-life and then support things like war and capital punishment." Indeed, I thought. This is certainly a journey of mixed messages, no matter how firmly we continued to affirm our inclusive design.

We tried to ease into the experience. Arriving in Washington on Saturday, we spent a few hours seeing the secular sites – the perfect activity after seventeen hours by coach. After a brisk tour of the National Gallery, Air & Space Museum, and the National Archives, we checked into our hotel and then sat down for the evening meal. It was then that the real focus of our trip began. Each student was given a rose – the symbol of the annual march – and asked to leave it wherever it seemed appropriate given the mission of our trip. They were asked to note in their journals their reason for leaving the rose where they did. After dark we traveled back to the National Mall, to the green space that flanks the Vietnam Veterans Memorial Wall. Perhaps it is a testament to the strength of that memorial that not a single rose was brought back onto the bus that night. Leaving a rose behind was a simple gesture, but their journal reflections revealed a complexity not apparent in the gesture: The students' grappling with the moral ambiguities surrounding the Vietnam War revealed a maturity and sophistication as they attempted to figure out what the value of a consistent ethic of life meant for them.

The next day we visited Arlington National Cemetery, where these young people were no less affected by the enormity of lost life which that hallowed ground represents. Again, their later reflections revealed the quiet, profound thoughts our students often harbor: "The cemetery is incredible... to see headstones just going forever. You don't realize how important life is until it's gone," said Deanna, a sophomore. Yodashorn, a student who joined our community from Thailand, added, "Every one of them is important, even though they don't all get a grave like JFK." One sophomore, Mary, offered thoughts that will stay with me for decades: "One of the quotes at Kennedy's grave said something about passing the torch. That made me angry. Racism, hatred... Don't pass me that torch; I don't want it. This is our country, we need to make a stand and fight for life." Junior Caitlin added to the sentiment: "People say you can't make a difference until you've grown up. We *are* growing up, and we're making a difference now."

These words uttered back at our hotel irked me; they brought me back to my earlier questioning. How exactly were we making a difference? Nothing would change tomorrow. Abortion clinics would still open, laws would remain in place. As I jotted down the thoughts my students had expressed, my mind wandered away from their reflection into the more turbulent waters of my own private thoughts.

From Changing What to Changing Whom

This precisely was the moment when I began to understand that student involvement in protests is less about changing whatever is being protested than about changing the participants. In a word, it is about transformation, about their learning. These students' thoughts that I'd been recording were the evidence. It was the change in each of these people (and in myself) that made the experience of protesting a form of service *learning*. These young people were experiencing the first step in action – a step that stood to whet their appetites for greater service. This change is appreciable. The profundity of this sort of change because it is more conspicuous than change on a more global, societal level can, in fact, be more moving. It is the change of the single human heart, conversion; and it is the very change to which Christ himself calls each of us.

Through the act of protest, students access other important aspects of service: an understanding of God, an understanding of other people, and an understanding of the self. Protest offers these opportunities in a unique way: students join a larger group of disparate people with a common goal. This experience of solidarity with others united in a common vision elicits from the students a sense of their own passions and provides them with a repertoire of methods for acting on them within the community.

The celebration of the Mass at the Basilica of the Immaculate Conception on the grounds of the Catholic University of American was another occasion for our students to make sense of their experience in a thoughtful way. "It [the basilica] seemed superfluous," noted junior Brian, "but as we looked around, they have a ton of smaller churches and shrines. As I thought about it more, I realized what a good symbol of God it is – huge, but personal." Brian's observation made my day: I realized that this trip to Washington, DC was an occasion that provided an opportunity for our students to attend to their conceptions of God, spirituality, and life in a way not available in the everyday classroom life back in Whitefish Bay.

The march itself was a study in humanity. Caught in the current of protesters, we felt the steady push of masses united around one purpose. The methods of our fellow activists were varied. Most groups' approaches seemed like our own: Most came together prayerfully and peacefully to make their voices heard under the protection of the Constitution. Some groups were more extreme, resorting to shock-tactics and frenzied screaming. A few groups had even arrived to protest our protest. Calling and responding to each other, my young companions marched for life and for each other, bearing witness to everything good and true and holding the torch of a new generation aloft, but with Mary's important, critical words about which torches a new generation is willing to take up and which are best extinguished echoing in our minds and hearts.

The nightly communal reflections mentioned above were a forum for our students' voices; as such they served as important resources that helped us all to organize the meaning of our experiences. Without time to sit, write, and discuss what we had seen and heard, we might have missed the "teachable moments" along the way. In fact, I'm certain we would have. As it turns out, these more formal occasions for reflection gave our students (and the adults!) enough time and space to think; and their thoughts became the focus of our prayer service during Catholic Schools Week, when Mary again summed up our purpose: "I am my brother's keeper. When we march in Washington, we're not marching for strangers. We're marching for our brothers and our sisters. We're marching for life." What more could we ask from a service learning experience? Such words reveal a greater appreciation of the world's ills, a greater appreciation of God and God's love, and a greater appreciation for the dignity of the self. These are the very things that inspire a hunger for justice in our students.

Conclusion

I am absolutely convinced that protesting is a sort of service. And our world, overflowing with injustices to be addressed, provides ample opportunity to engage in such service. Many schools like mine send student groups to protest the School of the Americas in Georgia; many send delegations to the March for Life; and many participate in smaller but equally moving protests against war, poverty, corporate disregard for the common welfare, and a host of other social evils which plague our local, national, and international communities. Until God is "all in all" (1 Cor 15:28), injustice will exist; because of that, we will always be called to serve others and grow in our own understanding of what justice is and how best to achieve it.

When organizing student participation in a protest, it is important to remember that the focus for the educator is one of introducing students not only to the injustice at hand but also to the presence of others who agree that something must be done. Students must be prepared ahead of time with the relevant facts, the teachings of the faith, and the moral logic that will later inform more direct service. As students begin to realize how God loves us and what God wants for the world, their appetite for more direct service to the most vulnerable grows and they eagerly pursue the opportunities for such service presented to them. Protesting against something is complemented over time by the demonstration *of* something: the love of God.

The word *demonstration* comes from the Latin word meaning "to point out." We use the word as a synonym for the word *protest*. We know, however, that there is another form of demonstration important for our students to engage in as Christians: concrete deeds of love in the spirit of Matthew 25. Students primed by sound education and participation in something larger than themselves become impassioned advocates who want to effect positive change in the world.

Our hope is that what distinguishes our students as impassioned protesters is that their passion is informed by their solidarity with those brothers and sisters they meet in their direct service *and* that their concern they express for the most vulnerable among us that at protests informs their direct service. In order for protesting to inform service and service to inform protesting, it is important for the adults organizing student involvement in the protest to keep the educational goals in mind as student participation is planned. It is vital that we remember what it is we hope students will know and be able to do when they return from the shared experience of a march or demonstration.

What will you do with your students when they return, full of enthusiasm? Do something, or risk losing that momentum. Provide them with a plan, an activity, or the opportunity to plan an event of their own. As in all matters of teaching, a certain degree of scaffolding and preparation is necessary. Supply that support, and you'll find your students growing in their estimation of the Catholic notion of justice more quickly than you might have previously imagined.

God raised Jesus from the dead, and the resurrection was the ultimate protest against the death-dealing values of this world! We Christians are swept up into the story of salvation, and we celebrate how Jesus' life of self-offering for the welfare of others demonstrates the power of love over hate, of life over death, of unity over division. By their baptism into this story that saves, our students participate in the great divine protest against hate, death, and division. With proper attention to what their baptism means for them, our students can participate in an important service: at once protesting against those things that injure the least among us *and* demonstrating the love of God.

Discussion Questions

1. **Principle:** What ways of talking about protesting seem most likely to be successful in terms of understanding it as a sensible response by Christians to injustice?

2. **Strategy:** In what ways can "protesting against" evil be framed as intimately related to demonstrating God's love?

3. **Try tomorrow:** How would you respond to members of your school community who oppose your students' involvement in protests because, they claim, students should not be involved in politics?

Resources

Vatican Council II. (1965). *Gaudium et spes: Pastoral constitution on the Church in the modern world.* Downloaded April 1, 2009, from http://www.vatican.va/archive/hist_councils/ii_vatican_council/documents/vat-ii_cons_19651207_gaudium-et-spes_en.html

Learning to Lead Through Service Programs: Examining the Notion of "Servant Leadership"

Jill Bickett

Having spent my entire educational life serving in Catholic institutions, I have had a lot of firsthand experience of serving and leading. When I was a child in my parish elementary school, my mother and father were always participating in school functions, attending the Altar and Rosary Society meetings, and working on various parish committees. I couldn't help but notice that my parents were almost always in charge of one thing or another, whether directing meetings, keeping the books, or making speeches to incoming members. Were they serving the parish? Definitely. Were they leading? No question.

In my high school years, I followed in their footsteps and became involved in my Catholic high school community as a student body officer. I organized spirit week, spoke to the student body about the mission drive, and spearheaded fundraising events. Was I serving my school and the student body? Yes. Was I leading? Absolutely. Later, in our role as young parents, my husband and I became very involved in our parish and in our children's Catholic grammar school. We chaired the parish carnival, organized the school field trip program, and coordinated the children's liturgy. Much like our parents had done before us, we provided both service and leadership to our community.

It is no surprise, then, that when I chose a topic to explore for my doctoral dissertation in educational leadership after a long career as a teacher and administrator in Catholic schools, I was drawn to the place where I had first come to understand what it means to live out my faith, the place where service and leadership meet.

Using research from my study, *A Case Study of Leadership and Service at a Catholic Female Single Sex High School* (Bickett, 2008), I hope to address in this chapter the connection between service and leadership, examining the notion of "servant leadership" adopted by many Catholic schools and addressing the dangers of gendered service, particularly in a single-sex institution. I will look not only at service associated with formal service learning programs but also other sorts of service associated with volunteering.

Service and Leadership: How Different Are They?

At first blush, the definitions of the words *service* and *leadership* seem diametrically opposed. Can one be a servant and a leader simultaneously? The examples from my life make me answer with a resounding "Yes!" And the same can be true for students in our Catholic schools. A careful look at the definitions of these terms reveals what these two concepts share. Service is defined as "any activity in which time is given to benefit another person, group, or organization" (Stukas & Dunlap, 2002, p. 412). Leadership is the process of persuasion or example by which an individual induces a group to pursue objectives held by the leader or shared by the leader and his or her followers (Gardner, 1990).

Both my experience as an educator in Catholic schools and my research convince me that opportunities for students to learn to act intentionally and selflessly for the benefit of others are also opportunities for them to learn how to persuade others to join them in their outlook and in their endeavors. Put briefly, opportunities to learn to serve are also opportunities to learn to lead.

This was certainly true at St. Marian's, the Catholic female single-sex high school I studied. Students spoke comfortably of the connection between service and leadership. When asked to address this connection, Amanda, one of the students, said, "A leader volunteers to serve everyone, and someone who volunteers to serve everyone is a leader." She believed that leaders "lead by example, go to Habitat [for Humanity] every Sunday, and encourage or inspire other people to help at a soup kitchen." Though Amanda identified service and leadership outside of school as working in social justice venues (Habitat for Humanity, soup kitchens, etc.), when talking about her work in the school community, she described her work differently: "Leadership is sometimes doing the grunt work that goes unnoticed or unappreciated, but just knowing that it needs to get done." This notion of leadership, that it involves working selflessly in serving others community, is embedded in many of our Catholic institutions, and is sometimes referred to as "servant leadership" (Greenleaf, 1970).

Servant Leadership

Catholic schools are places where the shared objectives of Catholic social teaching (CST) are part of daily life. Even though we can no longer assume that students attending a Catholic school are Roman Catholic themselves or that they regularly worship at a parish church if they are Catholic, we can generally expect that enrollment in a Catholic school presupposes some willingness to embrace and be guided by the philosophy and mission of the school. And a commitment to service stands as one of the most important shared objectives that Catholic school students are encouraged to embrace.

The notion of servant leadership embraces several concepts that align well with CST. Servant leaders, modeled on Christ, are those whose leadership embraces love and compassion for the sake of others and the world (Warneka, 2008). This other-centered definition of leadership suggests that the exercise of leadership have an end beyond itself, a higher moral purpose. In other words, *service* must come first or there is no need to lead. Further, servant leaders are concerned about building community (Spears, 2002) and are committed to the common good. Neither service nor leadership can be done in isolation; both require participation of individuals *in community*. A community founded on principles of servant leadership provides opportunities for students to envision a world where caring leads to action, and where service informs leadership – a place where *service, leading*, and *learning* are all intimately related to one another.

In my discussions with the students at St. Marian's, I found they had learned to identify service with leadership and believed that even the smallest acts of service were instances of leadership because these acts could also serve as opportunities for students to model service for others in their community. For instance, while leading the morning prayer at school, Molly reflected on the connection between service and leadership and the link to community: "Community is the window through which courage and character shine. To serve a community – to give oneself for the betterment of the group or the promotion of inclusiveness – this is the purpose of being a leader." Molly understood not only that in her service she acted as leader but also that the purpose of service is rooted in community. She had learned how closely related service and leadership are at her school.

One of the other significant elements of Greenleaf's (1970) theory of servant leadership is the notion that leadership, when tied to service, must never be self-serving and must always be collaborative. Carla, a senior at St. Marian's, wrote a reflection on leadership that illustrates this point:

Over these past four years I have learned to be a leader.

It means sometimes being willing to follow and compromise.

It means taking time to listen.

It means letting everyone see your imperfections, yet also your desire to improve.

It means being honest.

It means working tirelessly, and sometimes thanklessly, because you can see what needs to get done even when others don't.

It means sometimes admitting defeat.

It means exhaustion.

But it also means exhilaration.

Many of the items that define leadership for Carla are acts both of service and of humility. By her own admission, Carla learned over four years at the school that working for others and working with others in a transparent and altruistic way is one way to describe leadership.

The students I met understood the service ethos at St. Marian's very well. They embraced the notion that even "grunt work" was part of the job of a servant leader, and they spoke confidently of the school's commitment to service. Alba was particularly clear about the importance of service for each student's learning:

I think that the foundation of our school is service, and that it has influenced the actions of the whole school community – we're constantly collecting or going out and serving out in the community…. When you have a school whose whole mission was founded on the principles of service in the community, bringing gifts of time and love and spirit to the community, then that sort of permeates through every aspect.

Alba believed that St. Marian's was founded on service to others and that its students were provided both with numerous opportunities for service and with messages about serving. She spoke of service as "permeating" every aspect of the school's culture, and her use of the phrase "bringing gifts of time and love and spirit" evokes Christian notions that link a life of service to a life of faith.

The "right" kind of service provides opportunities for the students in our care to construct for themselves such a meaningful definition. Good service-learning programs help students learn to lead by giving them opportunities to listen honestly, to negotiate difficult situations gracefully, and to work hard. Learning how closely leadership and service are related gives our students a foundation for lives lived as agents of change, reconstructing the meaning of leadership from a competitive, personal drive for power to a desire to serve others collaboratively using "trust, respect, and unconditional love to build bridges and do what's best for the whole" (McGee-Cooper & Looper, 2001, p. 3).

A Cautionary Note about the Right Kind of Service

Encouraging students to embrace the servant leadership paradigm, however, is not without its perils, especially in a single-sex female school. Though some scholars assert that servant leadership is a genderless notion (Rhodes, 2001), feminist scholars contend that servant leadership can be a way of educating females to maintain the historically submissive role of "help-mate," which may amount to asking young women to consider leadership as a servile endeavor where their energies are spent in menial tasks rather than in visionary enterprises (Eicher-Catt, 1996). Female single-sex schools need especially to be aware of this danger and take measures to provide their students with opportunities for the "right kind of service."

There are service placements that can deliver the wrong message, particularly to young women. For instance, service that requires little skill and is tedious is not in and of itself an experience of leadership unless it is understood by the student as participation in an activity that supports the ideals of the community. Service placements should be chosen in part with an eye to how they might draw students deeper into the community. Without proper placements and a properly articulated philosophy of service, there is a particular danger that young women – who historically have been marginalized – will subconsciously view themselves not as servant leaders but merely as servants, thus reinforcing centuries old stereotypes of women's roles in society.

As part of the service program, students at St. Marian's were able to choose a service opportunity selected from an array of off-site programs that the administration had made available for them. The programs included service opportunities at Habitat for Humanity, Catholic elementary school sites, and food pantries. The majority of the students completed their service hours as aides at elementary schools, though the Habitat for Humanity site was amply filled with female students. Though the students that I observed at the elementary school sites were very happy with their service and very positive about their experience, I wondered what students would have chosen if there had been more service opportunities made available in addition to elementary classrooms.

My concern is that the traditional notion of "women's work" can be reinforced when service programs limit opportunities to stereotypical female professions like teaching. Gendered service is a danger in Catholic school service programs in girls' schools especially in part because elementary schools are such convenient placements. Other service sites that encourage female students to step outside traditional roles may be more challenging for service program directors to find, but the work establishing such placements is worthwhile because such placements provide opportunities for young women to explore other service and leadership opportunities beyond society's expectations, offering possible opportunities to inspire them to find their own way.

Conclusion

Catholic school service programs can be training grounds for a new kind of leader exercising a new kind of leadership. Using CST as a foundation and aligned with the practice of servant leadership, students can be 21st century leaders who support others, who value relationships, and who have the courage and faith to step out into the unknown (Warneka, 2008). The courage to step into the unknown is the courage to move from a hierarchical model of leadership to a more collaborative, non-competitive model. Catholic school service programs do best in this regard both when they foster a climate that values service and when they assist students participating in service to see themselves as leaders – and encourage them to act as such. Leadership without service is despotic, and service without leadership is anemic, unconnected to purpose and devoid of the power to create change. Helping our students to see the intimate connection between service and leadership – to see their service as *action with purpose*, linked to community – is a first important step in helping them to mature into healthy leaders for the 21st century, leaders who serve.

Discussion Questions

1. **Principle:** What ways of talking about service help students to see the intimate connection between service and leading – to see their service as *action with purpose*?

2. **Strategy:** Take an inventory of the placements available for your students to serve. What opportunities to learn the principles of service and leadership are present? What are the risks that learning inimical to CST might occur?

3. **Try tomorrow:** How might you start a productive conversation with students about the notion of servant leadership? Role play the interaction.

Resources

Bickett, J. (2008). *A case study of student leadership and service in a Catholic female single-sex high school.* Unpublished doctoral dissertation, Loyola Marymount University, Los Angeles, CA.

Eicher-Catt, D. (2005). The myth of servant leadership: A feminist perspective. *Women and Language, 28,* 17-25.

Gardner, J. W. (1990). *On leadership.* New York: The Free Press.

Greenleaf, R. (1970). *The servant as leader.* Cambridge, MA: Center for Applied Studies.

McGee-Cooper, A. & Looper, G. (2001). *The essentials of servant leadership: Principals in practice.* Waltham, MA: Pegasus Communications, Inc.

Rhodes, K. (2001). *The servant leader: Does gender make a difference?* Retrieved March 29, 2007, from http://www.eresultants.com/power_of_ser vant_leadership.htm

Spears, L. (2002). Tracing the past, present and future of servant leadership. In L. Spears & M. Lawrence, (Eds.), *Focus on leadership: Servant leadership in the 21st century* (pp. 1-16). New York: John Wiley & Sons, Inc.

Stukas, A. A., & Dunlap, M. R. (2002). Community involvement: Theoretical approaches and educational initiatives. *Journal of Social Issues, 58,* 411-427.

Warneka, T. (2008). *Black belt leader, peaceful leader: An introduction to Catholic servant leadership.* Cleveland, Ohio: Asogomi Publishing International.

Chapter 9

Icons of Service in a Catholic Context

William J. Raddell, Jr.   Martin T. Connell, S.J.   Ann C. Holmquist

Icons are part of our everyday lives. For most of us, there isn't a day that we don't click on an icon to open up a document or a program. The word *icon* is Greek in origin and means image or representation. A religious icon is an image that stands for a person or events. Catholics of both eastern and western traditions believe that icons serve as windows to the grace of God: They provide us a vision of God's love at work in the lives of people and re-present the lifesaving deeds of Jesus. It is in this sense that we present three modern disciples of Jesus, servants of the Gospel who serve as icons of what service in a Catholic context means: Dorothy Day, a founder of the Catholic Worker movement; César Chávez, a founder of the United Farm Workers labor union; and Jean Vanier, the founder of L'Arche, an international movement of communities where people who have developmental disabilities and the friends who assist them share life together in the homes they create.

In reading the brief biographical sketches that follow consider what principles discussed in the preceding chapters they manifest. How do they exemplify living the virtue of solidarity? In what way were they servant leaders? What marks their vocation to serve? How are their lives of service integrated into other areas of their faith life? How are justice and charity related? As you read their stories think of who the people are in your community who serve in a similar regard for your students? What opportunities do your students have to hear their stories?

Dorothy Day *(1897-1980)*

Anyone who has studied social justice has probably seen the graphic of the two feet of Christian Justice. One description in the first foot speaks about charity or works of mercy. The second speaks of justice or works of social action. Both are seen as essential elements of how we are called to live out Jesus' command to love. Love requires us not only to provide direct assistance to those suffering or in need but also to address the systems that contribute to their suffering or create a climate where the necessities of life that enable a person to live with dignity are missing. Love requires us to address and remedy unjust situations.

We see this dual focus in the ministry of Jesus. When Jesus is in the district of Galilee, he primarily addresses the immediate needs of the people he encounters. He feeds the hungry, heals the sick, sets people free of demonic bondage, and even raises from the dead the loved ones of those who mourn. When he is in Jerusalem, however, his focus shifts to addressing the systems that victimize people and exclude them from full participation in the life of the community. He asks why a widow should only have one penny to live on. He challenges the structures that place burdens on people in the name of religion. In the Temple he challenges the priorities of those who emphasize commerce over the respect that is due to God. He calls people to question their relationship with the social order and the compromises that they have made with an oppressive occupying government in response to the question of whether or not it is lawful to pay taxes to Caesar.

Catholic schools have done an excellent job of encouraging students to use their time, gifts, and talents to serve the needs of the "least" among us, whether locally or internationally. The challenge, though, has been to find ways to address the justice dimension through advocacy and other forms of social action. Often the faith community has focused on either charity or justice, finding it difficult to implement an approach that integrates the two dimensions. An individual whose life illustrated how one can achieve an integration of both dimensions of love was Dorothy Day.

Born in Brooklyn, New York, on November 8, 1897, Dorothy grew up in Chicago where her father was a journalist. His periods of unemployment gave Dorothy a chance to see how people experienced the sense of failure and brokenness that often comes with not being able to provide for their families. And her habit of walking through poor neighborhoods on Chicago's southside helped her to empathize with the struggles of others. These experiences with poverty, both personal and vicarious, fueled her idealism and a radical desire for social change. Safeguarding the dignity of people became a lifelong pattern in her life.

She became increasingly restless as a college student, dropped out, and moved to New York City, where she got a job at a socialist newspaper. Her sympathy for the plight of the working class, and her desire for such social changes as women's suffrage and increased workers' rights, and her opposition to America's participation in the First World War led her to join the Communist Party.

She followed the philosophy of free love and had affairs with several men. For four years she lived in a common law marriage with an Englishman, Forster Batterham. He found the notion of marriage distasteful of its connection as an institution sanctioned by religion. When Dorothy became pregnant with his child, he urged her to have an abortion, arguing that it was wrong to bring children into a violent and unjust world. She refused, having had an earlier abortion that she considered one of the most regrettable choices in her life. This decision helped to bring about their eventual breakup.

Though raised without a religious background and lacking any formal religious training, Dorothy always had a strong inclination to the spiritual, an inclination nourished early on in her reading an old family Bible she found in her parents' attic. She attended a variety of churches and religious services with friends. Though she embraced Jesus' message of caring for those around us and serving the least among us, she found the disregard among Christian believers for these very Gospel values a stumbling block to any deeper commitment to Christianity.

The birth of her daughter, Tamar, led her to reconsider this stance. She wanted her daughter's life to be rooted in values, and she felt that religion offered a strongest possible foundation in values similar to her own. She was attracted to the Catholic faith, which she saw as the church of the immigrants, the church of the poor. She loved the Church's discipline, its willingness to sacrifice and suffer, and its message of forgiveness. During the preparations for Tamar's baptism, she realized that it would be hypocritical for her to have her daughter raised in a faith that she did not share and so was herself baptized. After her baptism, she realized that she could no longer live with Forster and ended the relationship.

After her conversion to Roman Catholicism, Dorothy chose no longer to align herself with groups that openly rejected God, even if they represented causes with which she was sympathetic. Her spiritual life became rooted in attending Mass, praying the rosary, and reading the Bible. A profound awareness of her own sinfulness and of God's forgiveness led her to recognize the flaws in others without judgment: People sinned but were not evil.

Dorothy found herself longing to go further in her faith. She struggled with how to use her talents and abilities in a manner that would allow her to live out Jesus' command to love. The answer to her prayers seeking how were answered when she met Peter Maurin, a French immigrant twenty years her senior whose prayer and reflection had led him to a radical commitment to the Gospel message, like Francis of Assisi. He dedicated himself to Christ's mission to bring the Good News to the poor. He believed that the Gospel called for a radical response that would lead to the transformation of society. He found in Dorothy a willing listener who shared his vision of a just society that would provide what people needed to live with dignity. He became Dorothy's mentor and collaborator.

The Great Depression had left many without work, homeless, and hungry. The Communist party used these conditions to advocate the need for a socialist government. They published a newspaper, *The Daily Worker,* to promote communism as a solution for America's travails. At Maurin's urging, Dorothy used her journalism background and began publishing *The Catholic Worker* out of her kitchen in 1933. It sold for a penny – still the cost today – because she wanted it to be accessible to anyone. The paper highlighted the struggles of workers for meaningful employment and a just wage and social issues like poverty, war, and injustice – all examined from a Gospel perspective. The paper promoted the social teachings of the Catholic Church as a means of finding just and peaceful solutions to the problems confronting society.

When people came to visit or talk with her, Dorothy would offer coffee from a pot continually brewing on the stove. When she cooked soup, she offered it to all who were present. When people needed a place to stay, she offered them a place in her home. Dorothy saw in the faces of the poor and needy the face of Christ. This practice grew into the Catholic Worker movement's houses of hospitality, where people were offered food and shelter and welcomed into a caring community without judgment or coercive attempts to change them. Many of those who came seeking assistance were alcoholics and derelicts, but Dorothy pointed out that Jesus never made an issue of people's worthiness. His words spoke only of his identification with those who were hungry, thirsty, or in need of shelter.

Dorothy's unyielding commitment to justice created controversy and often led to friction with both civil and Church authorities. She was arrested numerous times for protesting against a variety of issues. Her last arrest came when she was in her mid-seventies when she marched with César Chávez in his efforts to unionize farm workers seeking just wages and decent living conditions.

She was a pacifist and felt that the Church's easy embrace of the just war doctrine was a departure from the early Church's understanding of participation in war as incompatible with the Gospel. Hadn't Jesus admonished Peter to put away his sword and warned his followers that those who live by the sword will die by the sword? She was vocal in her criticism of the Church in its apparent disregard for Jesus' counsel to love our enemies. How could one justify killing those who Jesus declared were our neighbors? Dorothy committed herself to the cause of peace, believing that this was the only authentic response to Jesus' declaration, "Blessed are the peacemakers." In addition, she criticized the Church she loved for its neglect of those in need and those marginalized from society when it was within the Church's power to advocate on behalf of these forgotten children of God

Seventy-five years after the movement began, those who have made Dorothy's vision their own continue to reach out to the poor and marginalized. Today there are over 185 Catholic Worker communities in the United States. The ideals of prayer, non-violence, simplicity, and hospitality that were the hallmarks of Dorothy's life continue to inspire those who model themselves after her witness to the Gospel. The issues that she was passionate about – anti-racism, justice for workers, war, and the dignity of the human person – continue to be the focal points of the movement's efforts.

Jesus' ministry focused on the proclamation of the reign of God. Too often Christians have equated the reign of God only with the afterlife and have failed to see how Jesus was speaking of our present day experience.

Jesus announced that the reign of God was at hand and could be found in our midst. Theologians speak of this reality as "already, but not yet." God's reign broke into the human experience with the coming of Jesus into the world, but it has not yet been realized in its fullness, where the divine is incarnated in those who have chosen to do God's will, who follow Jesus. Dorothy understood and embraced this vision. She wrote:

What we do like to do is change the world – make it a little simpler for people to feed, clothe, and shelter themselves as God intended them to do. And to a certain extent, by fighting for better conditions, by crying out unceasingly for the rights of workers, of the poor, of the destitute – the rights of the worthy and the unworthy poor, in other words – we can to a certain extent change the world; we can work for the oasis, the little cell of joy and peace in a harried world. (quoted in Miller, 1982, p. 98)

Dorothy believed that we do this both by addressing people's immediate physical needs and by calling for changes in the economic and political arenas that will enable people to live in the manner that God intended.

While Dorothy Day was alive many declared her to be "a living saint." To such acclamations she responded that she didn't want to be dismissed so easily. She considered what she did not the extraordinary virtue of a saint but the ordinary work of a Christian believer. She believed that what she did was simply to respond to Jesus' call to be his presence in the world, to reach out to our brothers and sisters in need, and to work on their behalf – something to which all of us are called.

César Chávez *(1927-1993)*

César Chávez was born near Yuma, Arizona, in 1927. His grandparents were ranchers in the area, and his parents owned a small local store. When the family business failed during the Great Depression, César's family moved to the family ranch. A severe drought forced the family to give up ranching, so at age ten César joined his family as they made their way to California in search of work. The Chávez family became part of the migrant community, traveling from farm to farm to harvest fruits and vegetables. César knew firsthand what it meant to arrive at the fields before sunrise to begin picking, to stoop all day in the full sun before returning after sunset only to prepare to do the same all over again the following day – all for meager wages.

He did not continue his formal schooling beyond eighth grade. In large part, his decision to leave school was based on his experience of discrimination there. The constant taunts of "dirty Mexican," the teasing about his accent, and the lack of respect for Spanish and for his family's practices and traditions were disheartening. At the same time, however, they made César attuned to the virtue of justice and the importance of treating others with dignity.

It was during his teenage years that César came to know the plight of the migrant worker more intimately. After his father was injured in an automobile crash, César went into the fields in order to help support the family. The conditions under which migrants were forced to work were appalling. The living accommodations were sub-standard: Indoor plumbing was rare; access to electricity was uncommon; and the migrant cabins themselves were more often than not dilapidated. The workers rented such accommodations from their employers, oftentimes at an exorbitant rate deducted directly from their wages.

Migrant workers had more to contend with than just poor living conditions. They also had to contend with corrupt labor contractors, agents hired by the growers to hire and manage farm workers. These agents, hired in part to distance growers from the condition of their workers, often underpaid the workers, keeping the difference for themselves. Another strategy they used to cheat the workers who were paid by the pound of produce picked was to under-weigh the harvest. César was not oblivious to these injustices, and he began to imagine what it would mean to change the intolerable working conditions of the laborers.

After serving in the United States navy from 1944 to 1946, César returned home to Delano, California. In 1948 he married Helen Fabela, and they moved to the Santa Clara Valley of California. It was here that César first met Father Donald McDonnell, who introduced him to the rich tradition of Catholic social teaching (CST). A young priest motivated by CST, Father McDonnell was determined to apply important papal encyclicals like Leo XIII's *Rerum Novarum* (On the Condition of Labor) and Pius XI's *Quadregesimo Anno* (On the Reconstruction of the Social Order) to the persistent injustices the migrant workers faced. He found in César a partner eager to use the Church's teachings to examine the conditions under which workers labored and in advocating for justice.

Along with the papal encyclicals, Father McDonnell gave César books about labor history and the writings of Gandhi. César noted the important role that the priest played in his life as an advocate for social justice:

Father McDonnell sat with me past midnight telling me about social justice and the Church's stand on farm labor and reading from the encyclicals of Pope Leo XIII in which he upheld labor unions. I would do anything to get the Father to tell me more about labor history. I began going to the *bracero* (guest worker) camps with him to help with Mass, to the city jail to talk with prisoners, anything to be with him so that he could tell me more about the farm labor movement. (cited by Nelson, 1966, p. 49).

César's reading and discussions with Father McDonnell helped him to see the situation of the farm workers through the lens of CST and to make judgments about the conditions of the laborers. What he lacked was a method for acting. That is until he met Fred Ross, an organizer in San Jose to recruit members for the Community Service Organization (CSO). CSO's goal was to help poor people assert their own agency. Fred Ross was an important influence in César's formation. According to César, "He did such a good job of explaining how poor people could build power that I could taste it. I could feel it" (cited by Ferriss and Sandoval, 1997, p. 43). In the two years following their initial meeting, César and Fred helped to organize community members to address problems like police brutality and discrimination. They led voter registration drives, started a credit union for farm workers, and helped them with such things as immigration and tax problems.

Msgr. Eugene Boyle (2005), an early collaborator of César's has offered his recollections of the years that followed. In 1962, César began to organize farm workers in Delano, encouraged by Christian churches. Three years later, relying on CST, he persuaded the members of his fledgling National Farm Worker Association (NFWA) to go out on strike against the grape growers. No one believed the strike would be successful. Because the National Labor Relations Act excluded farm workers from protection in efforts to achieve collective bargaining, it would take enormous strength to outlast the growers. How long could a union adequately picket 10,000 acres? How could the strength of impoverished farm workers compete with that of multimillion-dollar agribusiness?

The answer to just how workers could stand against the resources of the growers came in December of 1965: a consumer boycott against the products of one of the largest Delano firms. The NFWA representatives who were sent to the major cities in the country to organize and coordinate local boycott groups found their most hospitable reception in the churches. It was the following Lent that showed how fruitful the marriage of faith and justice can be. César began a 250-mile penitential pilgrimage from Delano to California's capitol, Sacramento, where he intended to petition the governor to do something about collective bargaining rights for farm workers. He considered the pilgrimage a sort of spiritual exercise for him and his colleagues to learn how to engage in a long struggle for justice. About the pilgrimage Msgr. Boyle (2005) recalled, "I saw the Spirit-driven Jesus of Luke's gospel steadfastly making his way to Jerusalem, consumed by compassion for the anguished he met on the way and expending his all to alleviate their pain."

On Wednesday of Holy Week, the pilgrimage halted because of the news that one grower had agreed both to recognize NFWA and to negotiate a contract covering all his field workers in the Delano area. On the following day, Holy Thursday, another major grower, known for his recalcitrance, succumbed to the pressure and agreed to hold union elections. On Easter Sunday, led by the cross and a banner depicting Our Lady of Guadalupe, the pilgrimage reached the state capitol. By this time César and his companions had ten thousand others accompanying them, "praying and pledging continued support for the cause of justice for farm workers" (Boyle, 2005).

The next two years were difficult ones as the NFWA continued to fight for recognition and elections and to negotiate union contracts. The number of contracts they were successful in negotiating is remarkable given the lack of protection of farm workers under the law. Many found the lessons about the long struggle learned in the pilgrimage to Sacramento difficult to bear and wanted to address acts of violence against the union and its members with violence, but César, inspired by the example of Jesus and of Mahatma Gandhi, went on a twenty-five-day penitential fast. He broke the fast with words that echo the Gospel:

Our lives are really all that belong to us... Only by giving our lives do we find life. I am convinced that the truest act of courage, the strongest act of manliness, is to sacrifice ourselves for others in a totally nonviolent struggle for justice. To be a man is to suffer for others. God help us be men. (cited by Ferriss and Sandoval, 1997, p. 268)

In 1969, the Catholic bishops of the country began to see the important role they might play in advocating for social justice. This was not without controversy because many of the growers were Catholic. The bishops' ad hoc Committee on Farm Labor was instrumental in the historic 1970 settlement between the United Farm Workers of AFL-CIO and twenty-six grape growers of the San Joaquin Valley. The victory was short lived, but there was no turning back: In the struggles that followed the bishops explicitly endorsed both the table grape and lettuce boycott. Inspired by the example of César, the bishops continued to advocate for the farm workers and their right to collective bargaining in the face of growers refusal to take seriously legislation protecting such rights.

In the years that followed, César broadened his goals beyond organizing for collective bargaining. He successfully advocated for a ban on the use of the backbreaking short hoe, for protection from insecticides and herbicides, and for access to drinking water and sanitary facilities in the fields.

César Chávez died on April 23, 1993, near his birthplace in Yuma, Arizona. His funeral in Delano attracted over 35,000 people from all walks of life, who participated in a four-mile procession that recalled César's earlier pilgrimage. For those who attended, it was an overwhelming experience of the influence of one man who saw the injustices around him and who, inspired by the Gospel, did something.

The Prayer of the Farm Workers' Struggle written by César is part of his legacy:

Show me the suffering of the most miserable
So I will know my people's plight.
Free me to pray for others,
For you are present in every person.
Help me take responsibility for my own life
So that I can feel free at last.

Grant me courage to serve others,
For in service there is true life.
Give me honesty and patience
So that I can work with other workers.
Bring forth song and celebration
So that the Spirit will be alive among us.
Let the Spirit flourish and grow
So that we will never tire of the struggle.
Let us remember those who have died for justice,
For they have given us life.
Help us love even those who hate us
So we can change the world. Amen.

Jean Vanier *(b. 1928)*

Jean Vanier's life is marked by searching. His search began early on when, as a teenager, he pursued a career in the British and then Canadian navy. It was during a trip to Lourdes with his father, a military hero himself (and subsequently Canada's ambassador to France and Governor General of Canada) that Jean decided to leave military service in order to continue pursue his search for meaning. His father's words to the chief of naval staff who was disappointed in Jean's decision to leave the navy best capture this new chapter in Jean's life:

> Jean's aspiration transcends the human level. Knowing him as I do, I feel sure that he is answering to the Master's call. As you have been kind enough to ask me for my comments, I can only say this is a matter between God and him in which man if possible should not interfere. (cited in Spink, 2006, p.30)

The Master's call brought Jean to join an international group of students gathered in France by Père Thomas Philippe, a Dominican priest, into a community, called *Eau Vive* (Living Waters), dedicated to growth in Christian theology, spirituality, and living (Spink, 2006).

The next many years were spent continuing on his spiritual quest for the place to which God was calling him. Should he be a priest? A trappist monk? A solitary? By the late 1950s he had decided to pursue a doctorate in philosophy at the Institut Catholique in Paris. His intellectual formation in philosophy had a profound influence on his conception of the Christian life. He has spoken of the deep human desire for meaning in our lives and the importance of concrete, lived experience over abstract notions and ideas (Tippet, 2006).

Before moving back to Canada to teach philosophy, Jean spent time assisting his mentor Père Thomas, who had moved from the life with youth at Eau Vive to sharing his life with men who were weak and powerless, who had been marginalized due to physical, emotional, or psychological needs. Initially, Jean was uncomfortable around the men, who were noisy and erratic in their behavior, but he had a sense that Père Thomas was on to something in the ways he had discovered the spiritual openness of persons with disabilities (Spink, 2006).

After teaching philosophy at St. Michael's College at the University of Toronto for a few years, he returned to France, where he again encountered Père Thomas, his spiritual mentor. As a result of their conversations, Jean became more and more distressed by the plight of people with disabilities. When he visited institutions dedicated to their care, he was horrified by the conditions in which these brothers and sisters were forced to live. He used his sharp mind formed by the study of philosophy and his sensitive heart formed by the example of the lives of people like his parents and Père Thomas to judge what he saw. Now it was time to act.

On August 5, 1964, Jean arrived at Trosly-Breuil, France, where he bought a dilapidated old house, christened it L'Arche (the ark), and invited Raphaël Simi and Philippe Seux to live with him and Louis Prety, another Canadian. Jean had taken Raphaël and Philippe out of institutions where they had been destined to live the rest of their lives. He did not know where this decision would lead, nor did he know if anyone else would be willing to help. What he did know was that everything in his life to that point had prepared him for the decision. He knew he had arrived at the place for which he had been searching his entire life, the place where God had called him. L'Arche was where his deep gladness and the world's deep hunger met (Buechner, 1993), and there would be no going back.

He soon realized that a welcoming home founded on solidarity and respect for human dignity resulted in Raphaël and Philippe's growth "in an astonishing way on the psychological, human, and spiritual planes" (Spink, 2006, p. 40). This led Jean to think of Raphaël and Philippe not only in terms of what had to be done for them but also in terms of their gifts and their potential to contribute to the community life they shared together. He discovered that they had as much to offer him as he could offer them.

The motivation for L'Arche was founded in Jean's religious faith. He wrote:

> If we keep our eyes fixed on [people with mental disabilities], if we are faithful to them, we will always find our path. We are constantly called to draw this love from the heart of God, and from God's mysterious presence at the heart of poor people. (1992, p. 7)

In this regard, it is clear that Jean drew his inspiration for L'Arche from the Beatitudes: "Blessed are the poor in spirit, for theirs is the kingdom of heaven" (Mt 5:3). L'Arche was founded as a place where every person is recognized as blessed even in their poverty of whatever sort, blessed with gifts to offer for the welfare of the community.

Persons with disabilities like Raphaël and Philippe have helped Jean and others without disabilities discover what it means to live in communion. Communion for him is marked by mutual trust and belonging. It is the dynamic, reciprocal exchange of giving and receiving; it is always deepening, always calling persons to mutual vulnerability and openness to one another. According to Jean, when we are in communion with others, we become open and vulnerable to them; and in this communion we become more human, more fully alive. We learn the way of the heart.

Jean Vanier's life makes it clear that the way of the heart must in fact be learned. He realized that approaching each individual with gentleness and kindness did not come naturally. He was a rigid person whose energies were goal-oriented. His goals had focused on efficiency, duty, prayer, doing good to others, and his philosophical and theological studies (Vanier, 2008). However, his life in L'Arche brought him back into the world of simple relationships, fun, and laughter. He found that persons with disabilities are masters who teach the apprentice how to live in the "world of celebration, presence and laughter – the world of the heart" (Vanier, 2008, p. 89).

For Jean, stories play an important part in building up community and are a prized activity at L'Arche. They awaken new energies of love and illuminate the way of the heart: "When we tell stories we touch hearts" (Vanier, 2008, p.90). Stories foster solidarity by revealing the reality of individuals' lives. When we hear the story of a person with a disability, that person is no longer simply a "type" of person; he or she is *this* person to whom I am invited to open my heart.

How we live with one another, how we receive one another in community in healthy bonds of love, has effects beyond our immediate context. Love transforms not only people present to us in our lives but also the world. In this regard L'Arche acts as a sign of hope pointing to what gives meaning to life. The communion of hearts in friendship, which is foundational for individuals who serve those who are weaker, gives meaning to a world in search of meaning. Living in solidarity – in friendship and communion – with people with disabilities, has helped him and his companions over the years to follow Jesus more closely. For Jean, his friends in community "are a source of hope, peace, and perhaps salvation for our wounded world: …If we are open to them, they lead us to Jesus and the good news" (Vanier, 1992, p.9)

Like Dorothy Day and César Chávez, Jean Vanier stands as an icon for learning to serve: His life in communion with the weak of the world demonstrates how humble service in solidarity with others through the grace of God becomes nourishing love, which is life for the world (Jn 6:51).

Resources

Boyle. E. (2005, March 28). Viva César Chávez! Viva la causa! *Faith doing justice: Blog of the Office of Evangelization, Justice, and Peace of the Diocese of San Jose, CA*. Retrieved January 31, 2009, from http://dsjjustice.blogspot.com/2005/03/viva-César-Chávez -viva-la-causa.html

Buechner, F. (1993). *Wishful thinking: A seeker's ABC*. (Revised and expanded,1973). New York: Harper Collins Publishers.

Coles, R. (1989). *Dorothy Day: A radical devotion*. Cambridge, MA: Da Capo Press.

Day, D. (1993). *The long loneliness*. Chicago: Saint Thomas More Press.

Ferriss, S. & Sandoval, R. (1997). *The fight in the fields: Cesar Chavez and the farm workers movement*. Boston: Houghton Mifflin Harcourt.

Miller, W. (1982). *Dorothy Day: A biography*. New York: Harper & Row.

Nelson. E., (1966). *Huelga: The first hundred days of the Great Delano Grape Strike*. Delano, CA: Farm Worker Press.

Spink, K. (2006). *The miracle, the message, the story: Jean Vanier and l'Arche*. Mahwah, NJ: Hidden Spring.

Tippet, K. (2007, December 20). The wisdom of tenderness: An interview with Jean Vanier. *Speaking of faith, with Krista Tippet*. Retrieved on September 12, 2008, from http://speakingoffaith.publicradio.org/programs/wisdomoftenderness/index.shtml

Vanier, J. (1992). *From brokenness to community*. Mahwah, NJ: Paulist Press.

Vanier, J. (1999). *Becoming human*. Mahwah, NJ: Paulist Press.

Creating Effective Service Learning Programs

Martin Connell, S.J.

The preceding chapters provide a broad outline of some important considerations necessary for establishing and maintaining an effective service-learning program in a Catholic context. This concluding chapter draws forth five common themes from the earlier chapters as a resource either for planning new service-learning programs or evaluating existing ones.

The earlier chapters have established that successful service learning programs situated in Catholic schools and parishes are marked by the following characteristics:

- Mission-driven
- Oriented to direct service
- Critical
- Focused on learning
- For life

In what follows I take up each of these aspects of successful programs.

Mission-driven

A service-learning program that is firmly founded in the mission of the parish or school is more likely to have a beneficial impact on the Christian formation of the students participating than one that does not. In this regard, the authors included in this book have illustrated the importance of engaging Sacred Scripture, Catholic social teaching (CST), and the local articulation of the faith.

We have seen the important role two foundational biblical texts play in this regard. Luke recounts how in the Nazareth synagogue, Jesus inaugurated his public life (Lk 4:16-21). Taking up the prophet Isaiah's commitment to social justice (Is 61:1-2), Jesus spoke to his hometown neighbors about his own priorities, about where and how he would concentrate his ministry: "The Spirit of the Lord is upon me because he has anointed me to bring glad tidings to the poor. He has sent me to proclaim liberty to captives and recovery of sight to the blind, to let the oppressed go free, and to proclaim a year acceptable to the Lord."

Matthew 25 is another foundational scripture on which to build service-learning programs. There is a story told of a little girl who asked, "If God is so big, and if God is inside me, then why doesn't God break through?" Why, indeed. It is this question that Matthew 25 confronts us with. Why is it that the love of God does not break through in our everyday actions? The scripture confronts us with the choices we – whom God has chosen to work in and through as members of the Body of Christ – make. Matthew 25 calls us to account for how we live our lives, what it means for us to love Jesus in the least of our brothers and sisters.

The tradition of CST is another important part of the foundation on which to build a service-learning program. The tenets of CST that deserve special attention include (1) a focus on the dignity of persons, (2) solidarity, and (3) justice. As Catholic Christians we believe that we are made in the image of God; this means our existence is marked by the Trinity. This belief points the way for us: We are meant for community – like the Father, Son, and Holy Spirit. Service programs should be prized as one way in which this human desire for community is satisfied. Our Trinitarian faith reminds us that the three divine Persons equally share in the Godhead – *in their diversity*. For that reason, service-learning programs should provide skills in recognizing diversity as a gift to be appreciated and not a problem to be solved. These beliefs impel us not only to serve but also to question social arrangements that do not recognize the dignity of humans or their equality.

Finally, a service-learning program should be linked to the school or parish's mission statement. Despite the recognition of the importance of service by many, there remain students, parents, and faculty members who need the reasons for such programs articulated in the most obvious ways. One important and effective means of doing this is to connect the goals of the program with local values as articulated in a mission statement.

To Be Considered:

- How do we articulate the reasons for doing service? Do we see our articulation as an opportunity to educate members of our community (students, their parents, faculty and staff, alumni, etc.) about service as a constitutive element of the Christian life?
- What are secular values that compete with the values that urge us to altruistic service?
- Which values do our program's policies and priorities support?

Oriented Direct Service

Because we hope our students will learn more about what being meant for community entails, it is important that service learning programs provide opportunities for *direct* service to the poor and disenfranchised. This is not to denigrate the important behind-the-scenes work that many volunteers do at non-profit agencies that serve the poor; rather, it is to underscore that one important goal for service learning is for our students to come to know actual poor people and learn about their tangible, lived realities. An important goal, as we have read in earlier chapters, is for students to see the face of Christ in the poor, the least of his brothers and sisters. It is impossible to accomplish this if students are sequestered in kitchens and offices rather than serving in dining rooms and streets.

Such service demands appropriate preparation. Many students who have not previously encountered poor or disabled people can be anxious about meeting them, fearful of the unknown. Likewise, many students who will encounter people they have come to regard as "other" arrive at service learning programs with racial and ethnic stereotypes and wrong notions about ability. In order to increase the chances that students will enter into a "right relationship" with those whom they will encounter during their service, a programmatic preparation suited to their needs should be in place.

Such a preparation could include, for instance, an overview of poverty in the United States. How is poverty reproduced from one generation to the next? It could also look at what it means to be poor locally. What is the situation of the poor in our city? Where do they live? Have they always lived here? How has "gentrification" affected the poor? Considering such questions assists students in beginning to see the situation of poor people.

Even better than researching issues concerning local poverty is the opportunity for students to meet someone from among those whom they will be serving before they begin their service. Organizations devoted to community organizing can be a helpful resource in identifying such a person; homeless advocacy groups can provide speakers to help students understand what it means to be homeless. The local diocesan Catholic charities office can be a helpful resource in this regard as well.

The approach advocated here can be envisioned as a trajectory that begins at the periphery (studying poverty as an issue) and moves to students' hearing the experience of poor people before arriving at the focal point, their service site. The preparation for service is "scaffolded." Each of the steps provides support for the next. One danger in attending to such preparation for direct service is to overstate its importance, however. If the preparation highlights the "otherness" of poor people and makes them objects to be feared rather than subjects to be encountered, it will have a deleterious effect contrary to the intended outcome.

To Be Considered:
- What are our criteria for choosing sites where our students serve? Have we formulated these criteria with our goals for their learning in mind?
- What do our students know about the people whom they will be serving? How do they know this? Does what they know "match" the reality? How do we prepare students before they arrive at their service sites?
- What local resources do we make use of? What are our contacts in the community? Do we insert ourselves into the life of the local church?

Critical

Service learning programs situated in Catholic schools and parishes should be critical. To suggest that a service-learning program have a critical outlook is not to suggest that it should encourage students to take on negative or cynical stances but rather that the program should foster an analytic sensibility among the students. We hope our students immersed in service begin to question assumptions about the status quo of the conditions of those whom they serve.

The Church offers us one way to pay such attention to the local situation; this way is detailed in Blessed Pope John XXIII's encyclical *Mater et Magistra* (1961):

> There are three stages, which should normally be followed in the reduction of social principles into practice. First, one reviews the concrete situation; secondly, one forms a judgment on it in the light of these same principles; thirdly, one decides what in the circumstances can and should be done to implement these principles. These are the three stages that are usually expressed in the three terms: look, judge, act.
>
> It is important for our young people to grasp this method and to practice it. Knowledge acquired in this way does not remain merely abstract, but is seen as something that must be translated into action. (paras. 236-237).

By helping our students see – to *really* see what's before them – and make sound judgments about what they see, we provide them with resources to begin to understand the circumstances of those whom they serve, providing knowledge for subsequent action.

One way to assist students to consider what is going on is to provide them with a very straightforward question to have in mind as they witness the conditions and situation of the people whom they serve: "Why is this (whatever *this* is) the way it is and not otherwise?" (Erickson, 1984). After considering possible answers to this question, students can take up CST as a rich resource to begin to formulate how the conditions might be different and what needs to be done to make them more just and equitable. A critical element of a service learning program, rooted in CST, provides a point of contact between service as an act of charity and service as a foundation for justice because it helps students to become more aware of their responsibility as citizens to promote the common good of all in all spheres of life.

To Be Considered:

- Can we discern the three elements commended by Blessed John XXIII in our service-learning program?
- hat role does CST play in our service-learning program? Are elements of CST taken up as tools for students' reflection on their service?
- What opportunities do we offer students to act as advocates for the people they meet in the course of their service? How do we help them connect Christian service to responsible citizenship?

Focused on Learning

Service programs should be organized for learning. Learning here is understood as the movement from experience to understanding. Without understanding, experiences of service remain episodic activities with very little meaning.

The principal resource for moving from discrete experiences to a more comprehensive understanding is reflection. Reflection is often imagined in romantic terms as what an individual does when she or he thinks hard about this or that experience. Many service-learning experiences take up this notion of reflection when they require students to journal or write essays about their experiences of serving others. Such exercises can help students to organize their experience, but they are more often than not insufficient for deeper understanding.

Though the individual is the locus of learning, learning does not take place in isolation. This is to suggest that conversation should play an important role in the movement among students from experience to understanding.

Experiences are a fundamental resource for understanding; and understanding, founded in experience, provides for the interpretation of new experiences, and so forth. In sharing our experiences in conversation, we invite others to search for, to grapple with, to organize meaning with us. Conversational storytelling among students about their service experiences can serve as a theory-building activity wherein together they along with adults jointly construct, critique, and reconstruct theories concerning the events of their service (See Ochs, Taylor, Rudolph & Smith, 1992). Chances for students to tell stories of their experiences provide them with opportunities to engage in the collaborative production of a vision (theory) of what happens in their service. As they listen to one another and question one another, students play a crucial role in advancing understanding; that is, in refining their vision.

Conversation among students is an important resource for their coming to understand not only what is happening to them as they serve but also how what they witness in service is connected to larger social structures. Where there is a sense of community marked by trusting relations and where opportunities for conversation abound, students begin to gain a sense of shared understanding which in turn enriches their on-going service and provides the stimulation they need to pursue continued personal growth. One only needs to recall the learning that Cleopas and his companion experienced on the road to Emmaus in order to understand the role conversation plays in learning.

If conversational story telling is taken seriously as a provision for learning and theory-building in service learning programs, knowing how to listen is a *sine qua non*. As Burbules (1993) notes, "Listening is an important aspect of legitimate authority, not only as a way in which one stands to learn something new, but as a concrete relational activity that alters the status of one's authority" (p. 33). Adults who consider the experiences of their students shared in their conversational tales as legitimate resources for understanding consider their authority principally as being at the service of their students' formation in the Christian life.

To Be Considered:

- What do we want our students to understand as a result of their experience of service?
- What resources are in place to help students move from experience to understanding? Is reflection perfunctory or is it a constitutive part of the service learning program?
- What opportunities do we offer students to talk with one another and with more experienced people about their service? How are the roles of the adults understood relative to student learning?

For Life

Service provides an opportunity for the Christian formation of our youth, changing them forever by complicating their previous understandings of the world in light of the Gospel and their experiences of serving. The Jesuit Volunteer Corps, a popular program of post-collegiate service, describes its participants as being "ruined for life" as a result of their experience of service and community. Likewise, our students' experiences of service carried out in light of faith and reason should be so transformative that they will never again be able to see things the same way. Our service programs should cultivate in our students a disposition to continue both to embrace opportunities to serve and to challenge injustices that they encounter. In that regard, service programs should be oriented to the length of life. Just as we hope to foster in our students a desire for lifelong learning, we also hope to nurture in them a desire for lifelong serving.

Our students should not think that "'out there' we do and 'in here' we think." When they are properly oriented to the breadth of life of our students, service-learning programs challenge such conceptions and provide a way for our students to live more integrated lives. Furthermore, well-conceived programs attend to the breadth of life in their concern for not only the practical and intellectual aspects of the lives of our students but also the affective and spiritual dimensions of their lives. Hearing the word of God and responding to it in the community's worship (both at Mass and in popular devotions and other communal prayer) affords students chances to situate their service in something larger themselves, the story of Jesus the Christ, the one whose life of self-offering is the life of the world.

Jesus provides the ultimate model for us in this regard. Our students' learning is obviously a principal concern, but the welfare of those whom they serve is wisely kept at the fore as well. It is not only for our students' benefit that they engage in service but also, of course, for the good of those whom they serve.

To Be Considered:

- What are the opportunities for students to serve outside of formal programs? Do we encourage our students' families to participate in these opportunities? Are there opportunities for alumni to engage in school-sponsored service?
- Have we articulated "throughlines" of service in our curriculum? What are the ways that we help our students to lead more integrated, less divided, lives?
- What are the ways that we underscore that service to others after the pattern of Jesus is a good in itself? How do we discourage seeing service as "résumé building"?

Conclusion

What have I done for Christ? What am I doing for Christ? What will I do for Christ? Those three questions commended by St. Ignatius Loyola serve as a fitting conclusion for this chapter because our ultimate desire for service learning in Catholic settings is that it be responsive learning. As Crowell, Caine, and Caine (1998) note, responsive learning

> is that which draws upon the interests and expressive qualities of the student; it is also that learning which takes action in the world around us. Responsive learning draws us inward to tap the originality and creativity of through and understanding. It also draws us outward, asking us what the responsibility of our knowing is, what kind of people we will be. (p. xiii; cited by O'Grady, 2000, p. 278).

Service learning provides our students with the resources to respond to Christ and his call and the provisions to follow him as disciples on the way. In order to inculcate this disposition of responsiveness effectively, service-learning programs must themselves be responsive to their charge to form the next generation of followers of Christ.

Resources

Burbules, N. (1992). *Dialogue in teaching: Theory and practice*. New York: Teachers College Press.

Crowell, S., Caine, R. N., & Caine, G. (1998). *The re-enchantment of learning: A manual for teacher renewal and classroom transformation*. Tucson: Zephyr Press.

Erickson, R. (1984). What makes school "ethnography" ethnographic? *Anthropology & Education Quarterly, 15*, 51-56.

Ochs, E., Taylor, C., Rudolph, D., & Smith, R. (1992). Story-telling as theory building activity. *Discourse Processes, 15*, 37-72.

O'Grady, C. R. (Ed.). (2000). *Integrating service learning and multicultural education in colleges and universities*. Mahwah, NJ: Lawrence Erlbaum Associates.

Pope John XIII. (1961). *Mater et magistra*. Downloaded on September 12, 2008, from http://www.vatican.va/holy_father/john_xxiii/encyclicals/documents/hf_j-xxiii_enc_15051961_mater_en.html

A Disposition Inventory

Katie Murphy, a teacher at Archbishop Carroll High School in Washington, DC, has her students do a "dispositions inventory" at the beginning of the social justice course that includes a service component. The assessment serves as a tool to help students and their teachers reflect on what was learned as a result of the class work and the experience of service.

What follows is a ten-point modified version of Katie's "Where I Stand." Students are invited not only to do the Likert scale but also to comment on each item in a couple of sentences. What other items could you add given your context?

	Agree				**Disagree**
1. Most homeless people are drug addicts, alcoholic, or mentally ill.	1	2	3	4	5
2. Most people on welfare are black and stay on welfare for a long time.	1	2	3	4	5
3. There is a direct correlation between laziness and poverty.	1	2	3	4	5
4. "God helps those who help themselves" is a Gospel verse that underscores the truth that if a person works hard, he or she will not be poor.	1	2	3	4	5
5. Poor people commit more crimes than others.	1	2	3	4	5
6. Food, clothing, shelter, education, and health care are basic human rights that should be guaranteed to everyone.	1	2	3	4	5
7. Poverty over generations can be explained by deficient character traits passed down from parents to children and/or by deficient genes.	1	2	3	4	5
8. Poor people have more children in order to get more government assistance.	1	2	3	4	5
9. Most poor families don't value education, which is the way out of poverty.	1	2	3	4	5
10. We can help poor people by using our interactions with them as opportunities to instill in them better values that will help them out of poverty.	1	2	3	4	5

Examen of Consciousness: Meeting Jesus in Service

Another sort of prayerful reflection seeks to discover the voice of God within a person's own heart and to experience a growth in familiarity with God's will. It is often referred to as the *examen of consciousness,* and is a prayerful way of discerning the movement of God's Spirit in our daily lives. The prayer takes fewer than fifteen minutes and can be done just about anywhere. It consists of three steps.

1. **Recall that you are in the presence of God.**

   Take a few minutes to quiet yourself, removing yourself from the crazy pace of the day. As you calm down, take into account how God is present to you. As you grow in appreciation of God present to you in your prayer, ask that the divine Spirit open your eyes to what happened in your experience of service.

2. **Review your experience in the presence of Jesus. Spend a moment reviewing any gifts of the experience that come to mind as well as any injuries done to you or by you to others.**

   Ask that you will learn and grow as you reflect, thus deepening your knowledge of self and your relationship with God and others. Ask Jesus to accompany you as you call to mind details of the service experience. Be concrete as you appreciate particular grace-filled moments that come to mind. Recall the voices of people you met, the smells that wafted through the air, the expressions on the faces of the people who were present. What did you receive in this experience? What talents, hopes, ways of being associated with you were brought to bear in the moment you are considering? Share with Jesus your thoughts and feelings about the experience.

   Stay with the events involved with service, dwelling on one principal question: How did I respond to God's gifts to me? How did I choose *that* course of action an not another one? Why? What helped or hindered me along the way? As you continue in the presence of Jesus to recall the service experience, consider how attentive you were to his presence during the experience itself. The poet Gerard Manley Hopkins wrote that "Christ plays in ten thousand places, / Lovely in limbs, and lovely in eyes not his / To the Father through the features of men's faces." Where did you see Christ's face?

As you become more aware of what you received and what you gave, give God the Father thanks through Jesus for the good done to you and for the good you were able to do for others. As you continue in the presence of Jesus and become more aware of how you might have hurt others ask God for forgiveness and for healing for the aggrieved persons. Likewise, as you become more aware of the ways others may have hurt you, ask God for healing.

3. **Looking back in order to move forward.**

Having reviewed this service experience, look upon yourself the way Jesus does: with compassion. Consider how much you need God's assistance and try to appreciate God's manifestations of concern for you. Give thanks for grace of these moments of prayerful reflection and God's enlightening presence and ask God for the grace to respond better to the Spirit's promptings in your life. Finish your time in prayer with the Our Father.

Resource

Aschenbrenner, G. (1972). Consciousness Examen. *Review for Religious*, *31*, 14-21.

Theological Reflection on Service

For many years Catholic educators have found Thomas Groome's (1991) shared Christian praxis approach a helpful method of engaging students in theological reflection. Here is an adaptation of the approach that echoes the "three stages which should normally be followed in the reduction of social principles into practice" suggested by Blessed John XIII's in his encyclical *Mater et Magistra* (1961, para. 236). This approach can be used to engage students in theological reflection on their experience of service.

I. **Describe the Experience – Look.** Tell the story of something that happened while engaging in service in as much detail as possible. Who were the other people involved? What was the setting like? How did what happen unfold? How did you feel at different points over the course of the event? Are there any images especially important to you as you recall what occurred?

II. **Relate the Experience to the Experience of Salvation – Judge.** What does the story of our Catholic faith bring to bear on your experience? Is there a scripture that relates to what happened? A scripture that relates to how you felt? How does Scripture affirm or challenge what you experienced? Is there a tenet of Catholic social teaching that comes to mind? What is the significance of the experience in light of the wisdom of our faith?

III. **Living the Faith Story – Act.** How will you respond in faith to what you have come to understand in reflecting on the experience in light of faith? Do you have a sense of anything God is calling you to attend to in your experience? As you imagine yourself in similar circumstances, how would you act? How will you respond to broader issues that this experience is an instance of?

Resources

Groome, T. (1991). Sharing faith: A comprehensive approach to religious education and pastoral ministry. San Francisco: Harper.

Pope John XIII. (1961). *Mater et magistra*. Downloaded on September 12, 2008, from http://www.vatican.va/holy_father/john_xxii/encyclicals/documents/hf_j-xxiii_enc_15051961_mater_en.html

The following resources are generously provided by Education for Justice... thousands of print-ready resources at your fingertips

www.educationforjustice.org

Education
for **Justice**
Web Site

...an essential tool for your ministry

Everything you need:

• Catholic Social Teaching Resources • Retreats and Reflections •
• Lesson Plans & Activities • Prayers and Prayer Services •
• Justice Calendar with resources • Current Events •
• Popular Culture and Media • Lectionary Reflections •
• Fact Sheets & Handouts • Signs of Hope •

Integration Checklist of Catholic Social Teaching and the Classroom

Integrating classroom learning with service experiences is often an area where critical work is still needed. Use the check list below to see how well your program is integrated into the life and mission of your school as well as with classroom learning. Check all that apply.

Our Service Learning Program...

☐ clearly states how it advances the mission of the school and its educational aims.

☐ has identified the places most critical for integration.

☐ has incorporated Catholic Social Teaching in its structure, vision, application, and analysis.

☐ has identified how we will promote personal development, intellectual/academic development, civic involvement, theological reflection and social analysis

☐ vhas connected service experience to the development of an understanding of how the Church has responded through its witness and institutions over time.

☐ has carefully analyzed the process to promote balance between the "two feet of a Christian" – the balance between charity – and justice.

☐ sets a core goal of building relationships between community members.

☐ places a priority on scriptural engagement, prayer, and advocacy.

☐ clearly involves students in the assessment of the needs of the community.

☐ fosters Christ-centered problem solving in students.

☐ respects adolescent development by differentiating goals and activities engaged.

- [ ] has taken into account the cultures of students and ways they are motivated.
- [ ] increases student's understanding of roles and responsibilities as a disciple.
- [ ] increases student's understanding of roles and responsibilities as a citizen.
- [ ] has identified what our desired student-based outcomes are.
- [ ] articulates clear expectations of students, faculty, and staff.
- [ ] identifies how to communicate new/revised plan to administration, faculty and staff.
- [ ] addresses how the program's requirements will be included in school handbook.
- [ ] has developed a process for parents to be involved and active participants.
- [ ] has anticipated the challenges or resistances that may be faced.
- [ ] has defined what our measures of success and effectiveness are.
- [ ] has reviewed our plan to identify where assumptions, judgments or biases are imbedded.
- [ ] has drawn on the research available.
- [ ] identifies ways to invite student feedback and critique.
- [ ] has carefully considered how best to balance academic rigor with experience-based learning.
- [ ] incorporate specific ways to invite students to explore reactions, feelings, biases, prejudices, judgments, experience and learn from them.

Education
for **Justice**

Service Learning Prayer

> *"Another world is not only possible, she is on her way.*
> *Many of us won't be here to greet her, but on quiet days*
> *If you listen carefully you can almost hear her breathing"*
> — Arundhati Roy, India

Leader:

This morning as we begin, we gather to step back and see the bigger picture, to place the work we do in the context of prayer and reflection together. We gather as one community, working to put our gifts, talents, and energy at the service of those who cry out for justice.

We come with a diverse array of gifts; we come with hearts and minds that are committed to the social vision of the gospel. As we begin our day together, let us take a moment to enter into silence and let go of all that crowds our minds and hearts.

(Pause for silence)

Reader: A Reading from the Gospel of Matthew: (Matthew 15: 9-12)

Then Jesus went from that place and withdrew to the region of Tyre and Sidon. And behold, a Canaanite woman of that district came and called out, "Have pity on me, Lord, Son of David! My daughter is tormented by a demon." But he did not say a word in answer to her. His disciples came and asked him, "Send her away, for she keeps calling out after us." He said in reply, "I was sent only to the lost sheep of the house of Israel." But the woman came and did him homage, saying, "Lord, help me." He said in reply, "It is not right to take the food of the children and throw it to the dogs." She said, "Please, Lord, for even the dogs eat the scraps that fall from the table of their masters." Then Jesus said to her in reply, "O woman, great is your faith! Let it be done for you as you wish." And her daughter was healed from that hour. Moving on from there Jesus walked by the Sea of Galilee, went up on the mountain, and sat down there. Great crowds came to him, having with them the lame, the blind, the deformed, the mute, and many others. They placed them at his feet, and he cured them. The crowds were amazed when they saw the mute speaking, the deformed made whole, the lame walking, and the blind able to see, and they glorified the God of Israel.

The Gospel of the Lord

Questions for Reflection and Sharing

- What disturbs you or challenges you in this reading?
- What are you hearing in this reading – what strikes you in a new way?
- Who is this woman crying out for justice in our world today?

Morning Prayer

Prayer of Intercession

Leader:

God of vision,

Open our eyes, and hears to see and hear in deeper ways.

Just as the woman cried out to be heard and her daughter to be healed, so we pray that our work may respond to the cries for justice in our world today.

We pray for those whose cries are ignored by the powers that seek to silence them.

We pray for those for whom life is unfair, for those who live in the midst of violence, for those who are killed, or those who lose their homes as a result of natural disaster, earthquakes, floods, volcanic activity, especially… (name)

(silence)

Compassionate God, we pray for those whose lives are cut short early by illness, or accident, or poverty, especially… (name)

(silence)

And we pray for those who mourn them.

All seeing God, we pray for those whose lives are made difficult because of the inequalities between rich and poor; the homeless, those who do not have adequate health care, or education, or jobs; for those who live in slums with inadequate basic facilities, the hungry and starving especially…. (name)

(silence)

Loving God, grant us the ability to use the talents we have been given to work in collaboration with others to change unjust systems, to persist in the face of challenges, to hope in the face of despair. Keep us focused on the bigger picture and remind us that your grace is working in us and through us to bring about your vision of the reign of God.

Concluding Prayer: (All)

God of Justice, May we resist the temptation to pursue our own interest, to preserve the status quo, and to participate in the conspiracy of silence which protects the rich and harms the poor. Renew our hearts, focus our vision, and strengthen our commitment to each other and the work we do in your name.

We make our prayer in Jesus' name,

Amen.

Education
for **Justice**

Prayer to Focus

John Bucki, S.J.

What is really important?
God, help me to focus on what is really important.
Help me to focus on what will give life.
Help me to focus on what promotes justice and peace.
Help me to let go of all the little things that don't matter.
Help me to let go of any legalism that blocks your spirit.

God, you are my Mother, my Father; You love me.
Help me to trust in your plan – your plan for life.
Your plan for the fullness of life for everyone.

God, you are the Spirit of Life for the whole world.
Remove violence from my life.
Remove violence from our world.
Teach me how to speak up for justice without violence.
Teach me how to learn from the poor.
Teach me how to serve with generosity and love
Teach me what I need to learn from those I serve.

God, help me to focus on what is really important.
Help me to focus on what will give life.
Help me to focus on what promotes justice and peace.

Education
for **Justice**

A Prayer During Food Drives

Leader: Let us quiet our minds and open our hearts to the reality of hunger in the world today. Take a moment to reflect on your own experience of hunger. When was the last time you knew hunger? How did it feel? Recall this feeling and let it unite you with all those who are hungry in the world at this moment. In your prayer bring your loving attention to human beings who are living at the edge of survival due to lack of bread, rice or even a simple meal.

Side One: God of Abundance, use our gifts, our creativity to eliminate the harvest of hunger that poverty has sown. Root out the seeds of greed and gluttony within the human heart that choke off the ability to recognize and respond to those who are suffering.

Side Two: Through Your grace, provide the nutrients we need to plough and plant, to tend and train the budding vines of compassion and care. May we hear and respond to the cries of millions of men, women, and children who hunger for life itself and are desperate for survival for just one more day.

Side One: Wean us from our normal diet of disregard and empty distraction. Help us to push back from the crowded table of self-preoccupation. Draw us instead to a common table where there is room and welcome for all, where all are fed.

Side Two: Help us to work to ensure that empty bowls be replaced by nourishing bonds of community so that no one is forced to beg at the edge of the road of life.

Side One: In places where war and violence are the cause of widespread hunger, call us to the inclusive table of peace and replace all fear and destruction with just ways to reconstruct security, home, and hope.

Side Two: May our actions and advocacy sow seeds of solidarity so that we might work as one body in Christ to eliminate the scandal of hunger, the politics of food assistance and the death of too many children as a result of starvation.

Side One: Bless the land and all those who work the land. Preserve us from drought and flood, from blight and disease. Grant all farmers increased yields, abundant harvests, sustainable production, and fair prices in the marketplace for these farmers, their families, and their futures.

All: Gracious God, nourish our world with hope and call your people to the table of cooperation. Bless our efforts to work for food security and eliminate hunger so that all might know a harvest of justice. May our attempts to end hunger not be politicized or prophesied, but realized in the sharing of our daily bread. We ask this in Christ's name.

Amen

Education
for Justice

Your Kingdom Come

Lord God,
in Jesus, you came in the body:
flesh of our flesh, bone of our bone.
We thank you that you did not remain an idea,
even a religious idea,
but walked, wept, and washed feet among us.
By your love,
change our ideas, especially our religious ideas,
into living signs of your work and will.

Through our lives and by our prayers,
your kingdom come.

Lord God,
in Jesus your body was broken
by the cowardly and the powerful.
The judgment hall of Pilate
knew your silence as surely
as your critics knew your voice.
In word and silence,
take on the powerful of the world today:
those whose words sentence some to cruelty
or unmerited redundancy;
those whose word transfers wealth or weapons
for the sake of profit or prejudice;
those whose silence condones the injustice
they have the power to change.

O Savior of the poor, liberate your people.

Through our lives and by our prayers,
your kingdom come.

Mark 15:1-5; John 1:14

Education
for **Justice**

Prayer for a World Renewed

O God,
our creator and sustainer,
we pray to you:
We want to celebrate life.
We cry out against all that kills life:
hunger, poverty, unemployment, sickness,
debt, repression, individualism,
abuse of the earth, injustice,
and all other forms of slavery.
We want to announce fullness of life:
work, education, health, housing,
safe environment, bread for all.
We want communion, solidarity,
a world renewed.
We hope against hope.
With the God of history,
We want to make things new again.

Education
for **Justice**

Prayer for Service

O God of great compassion
You have called us to serve the cause of justice,
and to be messengers of Your Good News
to the marginalized, the oppressed, and to all who suffer.

Help us to shape our passion, our talents, and skills
in order to transform the global community.

Bless us in our continuing formation as we minister to others.
Bless our hopes to work even more effectively for human dignity
and the fullness of life for all.
Bless our service efforts and each person we serve.
Open us to the Spirit.
In Christ we pray.

Amen.

— by Jane Deren

Education
for Justice

Food Drives & Justice Concerns: A Checklist for a Balanced Serving of Charity and Justice

How do we end the problem of hunger and food insecurity in the United States, one of the world's wealthiest nations? The scandal of hunger is a failure of justice. One common and increasingly popular way to address hunger, particularly during the holiday seasons, is to hold a canned food drive for a local hunger center or food bank. Those involved are motivated by the best intentions but may actually be making things worse. Canned food drives can provide essential items for shelters and hunger centers. But some would argue that food drives may actually perpetuate the problem of hunger by failing to address the root causes. Before you plan your next food drive, use this resource to take stock of the balance between charity and justice in your program. A few simple adjustments could make a world of difference.

Three Essential Questions:
1. How does your food drive balance CHARITY with JUSTICE?
2. How does your food drive foster greater awareness of the plight of hunger in your own local community and move participants to advocate for change?
3. How does your food drive not only provide food but build face-to-face relationships that enrich lives?

Steps to transform your program:
1. **Take time to reflect** on what you are undertaking and with what kind of spirit and motivation.
   Reflect on the nature of food and what it is you will be providing for those in need. Think about nutrition, taste, quality and the ability to choose for one's self.
2. **Encounter before action** – meet those who will be the recipients of your food drive first, before undertaking your campaign. Put a human face on the issue and encounter the realities that create hunger in the first place.

3. **Know the needs** before addressing them.
   a. Students should understand the context as they undertake their service.
   b. Engage and educate – explore the level of poverty locally and nationally and the reasons why are people hungry.
   c. Have students map the places in the community where people who are in need can go.
   d. Calculate walking distances, bus routes and fares to get from point to point.
4. **Pray all the way** – connect prayer and action. Read and reflect on the words of scripture that deal with feasting and fasting, of feeding the hungry and welcoming the one in need.
5. **Remove incentives and reward**s – challenge right and just motivation in responding with love as a mandate of faith – not the seeking of rewards for the "winners." No one should "win" because others are hungry. Have students provide creative alternatives themselves.
6. **Advocacy** should be as important as the numbers of cans collected. Can you get as many people to sign a petition to fight hunger and provide adequate safety net measures as you can get cans of food? Balance the two feet of justice.
7. **Reflect on the experience.** One of the most important efforts is to have students reflect and integrate what they have both learned and experienced. Reflection can be done individually or in small groups but should be an essential component of the service experience.
8. **Go the Extra Mile:**
   a. Plant a Community Garden – have students grow the food they will give, and their labor will be involved – ask the earth science classes to take charge of preparing the soil and selecting the crops to grow.
   b. Build relationships with sources of fresh and nutritious food like the local farmers. Cultivate community relationships that can work together to bring about lasting change.
   c. Think outside the box (or can) and get creative at exploring and address the issue on a variety of levels in a variety of ways.

A Check List for Analyzing Your Food Drive:

☐ In engaging students in a food drive, do students learn about the increase in emergency assistance as a result of cuts in assistance at the state or federal levels?

☐ Do students research and find out about the reality of hunger locally, among children, in the suburbs, among seniors and rurally?

☐ Do students address structural analysis questions: To what extent is the public sector responsible for providing a minimum of protection and care? In reducing or eliminating hunger related programs, is the government failing to shoulder its responsibility and pushing it off onto compassionate do-gooders? Is this movement a failure of public officials to provide safety net in securing life?

☐ Do you avoid reinforcing the "hero" mentality and instead reinforce the equal dignity of all and the mandate of faith as an ethic to care?

☐ Do students have the opportunity to build sustained relationships with those in need? Or is it "one-shot" service and out? Do those you are serving know you by name? Do you know them by name?

☐ Is relationship building a central part of the process? Do students do more than just "serve the hungry"? Do they sit with them and share a meal as equals?

☐ Do you reinforce respect and human dignity by considering the nutritional needs and tastes of those served and by sorting out items that are expired, damaged or spoiled?

☐ Do students have an opportunity to do experiential learning by putting themselves in someone else's shoes? Are students invited and encouraged to experience their own hunger in order to appreciate the body's need for food? Can they live on a food stamp budget for a week? a month? Can they experience going without a meal, or getting from shelter to shelter on their own? (Consider integrating Catholic Relief Services (CRS) "FoodFast" program into the structure of your drive.)

☐ Do students learn from those they are serving about the causes and consequences of hunger?

☐ Do students have an opportunity to explore the connection between hunger issues locally, nationally and globally?

☐ Does your food drive build up the student's sense of discipleship and responsibility for one's neighbor in a loving and holistic way?

☐ Is the right motivation built in and fostered in your drive by avoiding incentives, competition and rewards for winners?

☐ Do you build in "See, Judge, Act" into the process?

☐ Do you integrate advocacy into the food drive? – locally, state-wide and nationally?

☐ Do you have a clear vision of the model of justice that is operative in the structure and implementation of your food drive?

☐ Upon completion of the drive, do you take time to have students reflect upon, journal and discuss their experience of the food drive and the insights they have gained?

Education
for **Justice**

Service Learning Planning Worksheets

> *Jesus summoned them and said, "You know that the rulers of the Gentiles lord it over them, and the great ones make their authority over them felt. But it shall not be so among you. Rather, whoever wishes to be great among you shall be your servant; whoever wishes to be first among you shall be your slave. Just so, the Son of Man did not come to be served but to serve and to give his life as a ransom for many."*
> — Matthew 20:25-28

One of Mother Teresa's best-known sayings is: "The fruit of Love is Service and the fruit of Service is Peace."[1]

Through the experience of service, may we have the eyes to see the true humanity and inherent dignity of the people before us.

May we attune ourselves to the call of the gospel to respond as Jesus taught us. May we heed the call to serve with great love and remember:

Jesus is the Word – to be spoken.
Jesus is the Life – to be lived.
Jesus is the Love – to be loved.
Jesus is the Joy – to be shared.
Jesus is the Sacrifice – to be offered.
Jesus is the Peace – to be given.
Jesus is the Bread of life – to be eaten.
Jesus is the Hungry – to be fed.
Jesus is the Thirsty – to be satiated.
Jesus is the Naked – to be clothed.
Jesus is the Homeless – to be taken in.
Jesus is the Sick – to be healed.
Jesus is the Lonely – to be loved.

Amen.

[1] Mother Teresa of Calcutta, *A Fruitful Branch on the Vine, Jesus.* St. Anthony Messenger Press, Cincinnati, Ohio, 2000, p. 36

Fill in the information below to develop a holistic vision for your service learning program.

Mission Statement of School:

_____

_____

_____

_____

Connection to Mission: Identify how your service learning program is carrying out the mission of your school:

_____

_____

_____

_____

Vision & Motivation: Why are your students doing service? What is your vision for your service program?

_____

_____

_____

_____

Core values behind your service program:

- _____
- _____
- _____
- _____

Three Key Goals of Your Service Learning Program

Identify the top three goals of your service learning program. In setting goals identify goals in the planning and preparation phase, in the implementation phase, and after the experience. Use the Goal Setting Worksheet below to identify timelines and persons responsible for each goal. Print as many copies as needed.

Goal 1: BEFORE (setting the tone, preparing and engaging students)

_____

_____

_____

_____

Goal 2: DURING (how students will encounter and experience those they are in relationship with during the service learning experience)

_____

_____

_____

_____

Goal 3: AFTER (what you will do to assist students in exploring and reflecting on their experience afterwards)

_____

_____

_____

_____

Goal Setting Worksheet

Goal # ____

Action Steps required:	Person Responsible/ Collaboration Required	Deadline
1.		
2.		
3.		
4.		
5.		
6.		
7.		

Notes:

Appendix L

Name *YOUR* Challenges Worksheet

Service learning experiences are powerful opportunities for growth and insight. They can provide all involved with life changing encounters, but in order for this to be the case, careful planning is needed. One important element of planning is to anticipate the challenges ahead of time so that you have the capacity to prevent these from detracting from the overall experience. Take some time to carefully consider the realistic challenges and the possibilities or solutions that can support your efforts and lead to the desired goals.

Q: What challenges exist that could affect your overall plan?

Stakeholders	Challenges – anticipated, perceived or actual:	How you will address the challenges by brainstorming possible solutions, & Strategic Options
from those being served:		
from the service sites:		
from students:		
from parents:		
from faculty:		
from administration:		
from others:		

Jill Bickett is an education professional with a distinguished career of leadership and service in Catholic schools.

Martin Connell is a Jesuit priest serving as an assistant professor in the School of Education at Loyola Marymount University, Los Angeles, California.

Christiane Connors works at the National Catholic Educational Association (NCEA) in Washington, DC and directs the secondary schools department's publications.

Katherine Feely is a sister of Notre Dame (SND) from Cleveland, OH and directs the Education for Justice Project at the Center of Concern in Washington, DC.

Ann Conley Holmquist currently serves as co-director of the Office for Adult Spirituality at Loyola High School, Los Angeles, California.

Michael Lee is a Jesuit priest and an assistant professor of Religious Education in the Department of Theological Studies at Loyola Marymount University, Los Angeles, California.

Katie Murphy is a social justice teacher at Archbishop Carroll High School in Washington, D.C.

William Raddell, Jr. teaches religion at Villa Angela-St. Joseph High School in Cleveland, Ohio.

James Skerl is chair of the theology department at St. Ignatius High School in Cleveland, Ohio.

Christian Tomsey teaches English at Dominican High School in Whitefish Bay, Wisconsin.

JoEllen Windau Cattapan formerly served as associate director of Catholics on Call and presently contracts with Charis Ministries to evaluate young adult retreat programs.